Communion

By Aidan Mathews

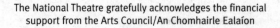
The National Theatre gratefully acknowledges the financial
support from the Arts Council/An Chomhairle Ealaíon

Communion

By Aidan Mathews

Communion by Aidan Mathews was first performed at the Peacock Theatre, Dublin on 25 April 2002. Press night was 1 May 2002.

The play takes place in the late 90s in a fashionable Dublin suburb

There will be one interval of 15 minutes

Cast in order of appearance

Jordan McHenry	Peter Hanly
Marcus McHenry	Frank McCusker
Martha McHenry	Stella McCusker
Arthur McLoughlin	Bosco Hogan
Fr. Anthony O'Driscoll	Peter Gowen
Felicity Spellman	Janet Moran

Director	Martin Drury
Designer	Francis O'Connor
Lighting Designer	Rupert Murray
Sound	Cormac Carroll
Stage Director	Finola Eustace
Assistant Stage Manager	Stephen Dempsey
Voice Coach	Andrea Ainsworth
Set	Abbey Theatre Workshop
Costumes	Abbey Theatre Wardrobe Department

Please note that the text of the play which appears in this volume may be changed during the rehearsal process and appear in a slightly altered form in performance.

Aidan Mathews *Author*

Aidan Mathews was born in Dublin in 1956. He was educated at University College Dublin, Trinity College and at Stanford University where he studied under the philosopher and theologian Rene Girard. He has published three collections of poetry, **Windfalls** (Dolmen), **Minding Ruth** (Gallery) and **According to the Small Hours** (Cape); a novel, **Muesli at Midnight** (Secker&Warburg) and two collections of short stories, **Adventures in a Bathyscope** (S&W), which won the Sunday Tribune Literature Award and was shortlisted for the GPA Award, and **Lipstick on the Host** (Cape) which won Italy's Cavour Prize for Foreign Fiction. He has written a number of plays, among them a one-woman show **The Diamond Body**, for which actress Olwen Fouere won a Jacob's Award, **The Antigone** at the Project, **Exit-Entrance** (Sunday Tribune Theatre Award, Gallery Press) in the Peacock, and a translation of **The House of Bernarda Alba** by Lorca for the Gate. His books have been translated into French, German, Italian and Dutch.

Martin Drury *Director*

Martin has directed productions for Second Age, Opera Theatre Company and Druid Theatre where he was script editor (1990-1993), but he is best known for his development of new work for young audiences as Artistic Director of TEAM (1981-1985) and Founder-Director of The Ark (1992-2001). He has worked closely with leading Irish playwrights, commissioning and directing plays by Bernard Farrell, John McArdle, Frank McGuinness and Jim Nolan. During his period as Director, The Ark won the Irish Times/ESB Judges' Special Award (1998) and was nominated for Best Company Award (2000). His current work outside theatre includes being Environment (Design and Arts) Adviser for the new Mater and Children's Hospital Development. He is an Associate Director of the National Theatre and is Honorary Fellow of the Department of Psychology (UCD).

Francis O'Connor *Designer*

Francis trained at Wimbledon School of Art. Previous work at the Abbey and Peacock Theatres includes **Silverlands, She Stoops to Folly, The Importance of Being Earnest, The Wake** which toured to the Edinburgh Festival, **Toupees and Snare Drums**, CoisCéim/Abbey Theatre co-production, **Tarry Flynn** and **The Colleen Bawn** which toured to the Royal National Theatre, London, **The Freedom of the City** which toured to the Lincoln Center, New York, **The House, Iphigenia at Aulis** and **Big Maggie**. Work with Druid Theatre Company includes **My Brilliant Divorce, The Beauty Queen of Leenane**, which toured to Royal Court Theatre and Broadway, **The Lonesome West**, Broadway, **The Leenane Trilogy, The Way You Look Tonight** and **The Country Boy**. Other theatre work includes Arthur Miller's **Mr Peter's Connections**, Signature, New York, **Love upon the Throne**, Comedy Theatre, West End, **Two Pianos, Four Hands**, Birmingham Rep, **After Easter**, RSC, **The Clearing**, Bush Theatre, **Sacred Heart**, Royal Court, and **Closer**, Royal

National Theatre and tour, **Peer Gynt,** Royal National Theatre, **The Weir,** Canadian Stage Company, **A Small Family Business,** Chichester Festival. Music theatre includes **Enter the Guardsman,** Donmar Warehouse, **La Vie Parisienne,** D'Oyly Carte and **May Night,** Wexford Festival, **La Cava,** West End and **Honk,** Tel Aviv. Most recently he designed **The Lieutenant of Inishmore,** RSC and **A Raisin in the Sun,** Young Vic. Francis won the Irish Times/ESB Best Designer Award 1997 for **Tarry Flynn** and **The Leenane Trilogy** and won it again in 2001 for **Big Maggie** and **Iphigenia at Aulis.**

Rupert Murray *Lighting Designer*

Rupert is a freelance lighting designer and producer. Recent lighting designs include **Lovers at Versailles, A Whistle in the Dark, The Gigli Concert** and **Famine,** for the Murphy Festival, Jim Nolan's **Blackwater Angel,** Brian Friel's **Translations,** Abbey Theatre, Shelagh Stephenson's **The Memory of Water** for the Peacock Theatre, Neil LaBute's **bash** and Noel Coward's **Blithe Spirit** at the Gate Theatre, as well as their touring productions of Samuel Beckett's **I'll Go On, Waiting for Godot** and **Krapp's Last Tape.** He is the lighting designer of **Riverdance - The Show** which is currently touring the USA and Europe. Rupert was Festival Director of the St Patrick's Festival from 1995 to 1999 and was a key member of the team which transformed Ireland's national celebrations. He has also been responsible for staging and directing the opening and closing festivities at the Wexford Festival Opera for the last three years. Through his company Creative Events he produces and stages major corporate, civic and theatrical events all around Ireland.

Peter Gowen *Fr. Anthony O'Driscoll*

Peter's appearances at the Abbey and Peacock theatres include **Observe The Sons of Ulster Marching towards the Somme,** Barbican London, European and UK Tour, **A Whistle in the Dark, A Child's Christmas in Wales, Madigan's Lock** and **Shadow of a Gunman.** Other theatre work includes **Death of a Salesman, Philadelphia Here I Come!, Translations, Fathers and Sons** Gaiety Theatre, **A Touch of the Poet, The Country Boy, The Beauty Queen of Leenane, Werewolves, At the Black Pig's Dyke,** Druid Theatre Company, **Bedbound,** Dublin Theatre Festival 2000, **Someone to Watch over Me,** Drum Theatre, **The Plough and The Stars,** UK tour and West End, **A Doll's House,** UK tour, West End and Broadway, **Juno and the Paycock,** UK tour and West End, **The Forest, Mutabilitie** and **Making History,** Royal National Theatre. Television credits include **Paradise Club,** BBC, **Minder,** ITV, **Coronation Street,** ITV and **On Home Ground,** RTE. Films include **Eat the Peach, The Butcher Boy, Dancing at Lughnasa** and **A Love Divided.**

Peter Hanly *Jordan*

Peter was a member of Dublin Youth Theatre before joining Theatre Unlimited where he worked as a company member for two years. Theatre work includes **Big Maggie** and **Sive,** Abbey Theatre, **Kvetch,** Kilkenny Arts Festival, **Three Days of Rain, The School for Scandal, Down Onto Blue, The**

Way of the World and **Digging for Fire**, all with Rough Magic Theatre Company, **The Promise** and **The Lonesome West**, the Liverpool Everyman, **Making Noise Quietly** with the Oxford Stage Company on tour in Britain and in the West End, London, **Love Me!?**, **Car Show**, Corn Exchange, **The Gay Detective**, Project Arts Centre and Tricycle Theatre, London, **The Seagull** and **The Breadman**, Gate Theatre, **Lovechild**, Project Arts Centre, **The Ash Fire**, Pigsback Theatre Company, Project Arts Centre and Tricycle, **The Conquest of the South Pole**, Theatre Demo, **A Life**, Olympia Theatre, **Translations** and **Bent**, Red Kettle Theatre Company. His film and television work includes **Black Day at Black Rock**, Venus Productions/RTE, **Ballykissangel**, World Productions/BBC, **First Communion Day**, Tigerlilly Films/BBC, **Jumpers**, G & H Productions/BBC, **Guiltrip**, Temple Films, **Braveheart**, Icon Productions and **The Truth About Claire**, RTE.

Bosco Hogan *Arthur*

Bosco began his acting career with the RTE Repertory Company before joining the Abbey Company for a four year-stay. Among his favourite roles there are Young Brendan Behan in **Borstal Boy**, Public Gar in **Philadelphia, Here I Come!**, Tarry in **Tarry Flynn**, Tom in **The Glass Menagerie**, Piper in **Observe the Sons of Ulster Marching Towards the Somme** and Brendan Behan in **Borstal Boy**. More recently Bosco played the villainous Mr. Corrigan in Conall Morrison's production of **The Colleen Bawn**, a big hit at both the Abbey and at the National Theatre in London, Dr Dodds in **The Freedom of the City** which toured to the Lincoln Center, New York and Alonso in **The Tempest**. London stage roles include Edmund in **King Lear** at the Young Vic, Delio in **The Duchess of Malfi** at the Roundhouse and at Manchester's Royal Exchange and Richard Greatham in **Hay Fever**. Many appearances on British television include Jonathan Harker in **Count Dracula**, Edward Ferrars in **Sense and Sensibility** (BBC), Sir Paul Berowne in P D James's **A Taste for Death**, several appearances in **Tales of the Unexpected**, DCC Wesley Morton in the series **The Chief** (Anglia), Dr Michael Ryan in **Ballykissangel** (BBC) and Detective Inspector Gerry Cody in **Making the Cut** (RTE). Films include **The General, Sweeney Todd, Some Mother's Son, Kidnapped, In the Name of the Father, Zardoz, Race for Survival** (Disney), **The Magnificent Ambersons** and Stephen Dedalus in **A Portrait of the Artist as a Young Man**. His one-man show **I Am of Ireland**, a maginifcent portrayal of W B Yeats which toured Ireland, England, Italy, Romania, Bulgaria and the USA was recently released on video.

Frank McCusker *Marcus*

Frank's appearances at the Abbey and Peacock Theatres include **The Sanctuary Lamp, Translations, The House, The Tempest, The Importance of Being Earnest, She Stoops to Folly, As the Beast Sleeps, Observe the Sons of Ulster Marching Towards the Somme, Shay Mouse, The Third Law of Motion, The Last Apache Reunion, The Playboy of the Western World** (Helen Hayes

Award in Washington DC), **The Glass Menagerie, The Gentle Island** and **The Lower Depths**. Other theatre work includes **Aristocrats**, Gate Theatre and Lincoln Center, New York, **Life Support** (directed by Harold Pinter), Aldwych Theatre, West End, **Torchlight and Laserbeams**, Gaiety Theatre and Edinburgh International Festival, **Wild Harvest**, Druid Theatre, Gaiety Theatre, **Moonshine**, Red Kettle and Abbey Theatre, **Equus**, Gaiety Theatre, **Hamlet** and **King Lear**, Second Age Productions, **The Man with the Flower in his Mouth**, Project Arts Centre, **The Collection**, Gate Theatre. Television and films include **The Railway Station Man, Getting Hurt, Out of Hours, Dear Sarah, J J Biker, Agnes Brown, Rebel Heart, David Copperfield, Day One, As the Beast Sleeps** and **The Affair of the Necklace**.

Stella McCusker *Martha*

Stella's previous performances at the Abbey and Peacock Theatres include **Philadelphia, Here I Come!,The Mai, Portia Coughlan** and **Treehouses**. She has worked extensively in Ireland and the UK including the Royal Shakespeare Company, the Royal Court, London, Royal Exchange Theatre, Manchester, Glasgow Citizens, the Lyceum, Edinburgh, Almeida, London, Druid Theatre, Galway, Gate Theatre, Dublin and Lyric Theatre, Belfast. She appeared on Broadway in Joe Dowling's production of **Juno and the Paycock**, at the world Theatre Festival Toronto in Druid's production of **At the Black Pig's Dyke** and at the National Theatre, Oslo in the Lyric Theatre production of Ibsen's **Ghosts** as Mrs Alving. More recently she appeared in **Convictions**, Tinderbox Theatre Company, **Coronation Voyage**, Prime Cut Productions, and **Our Father**, Almeida Theatre. Film and television credits include **On Home Ground, Making the Cut, Mia Mine Forever, Errors and Omissions, So You Think You've Got Troubles, Foreign Bodies, Troubles, The Governor, Lovejoy, You, Me and Marley, Snakes and Ladders, The Playboys, Act of Betrayal, This is the Sea** and **Dear Sarah** for which she received a Jacobs Award. She is a regular broadcaster on BBC Radio Drama.

Janet Moran *Felicity*

Previous performances at the Abbey and Peacock Theatres include **The Barbaric Comedies, The Well of the Saints** and **The Hostage**. Other theatre work includes **Royal Supreme,** Theatre Royal, Plymouth, **Guess Who's Coming to the Dinner,** Calypso Productions, **Dead Funny,** Rough Magic Theatre Company, **Playing from the Heart,** The Ark, **Love and Understanding,** Purple Heart Theatre Company, **Romeo and Juliet, Othello,** Second Age Theatre Company, **Emma,** Storytellers, **The Stomping Ground,** Red Kettle, **Stella by Starlight,** Gate Theatre, **Her Big Chance,** Bewley's Theatre Company, **Car Show,** Corn Exchange and **Xaviers,** Calipo Theatre Company of which she is an associate member, which was nominated for best production at the 1999 Irish Times/ESB Theatre Awards. Film and television credits include **Career Opportunities** (RTE/BBC), **Fair City, Nothing Personal, Moll Flanders** and **The Butcher Boy.**

Amharclann Na Mainistreach
The National Theatre

Amharclann Na Mainistreach
The National Theatre

The National Theatre
The Abbey and Peacock Theatres

Since its formation as the National Theatre of Ireland
by W B Yeats and Lady Augusta Gregory in 1904,
the Abbey Theatre has been the cradle of new drama in
Ireland for successive generations of Irish playwrights.
From the early works of Synge and O'Casey, through to
those writers at the cutting edge of Irish theatre today,
new plays have remained at the very core of the
Abbey's artistic policy and have helped to establish and
maintain its reputation as Ireland's foremost cultural
institution.

COMMUNION

Aidan Mathews

For Lucy
at last

Inter faeces et urinam nascimur.
(We are born amid shit and piss.)

Saint Augustine

Characters

JORDAN McHENRY, *a young man who is dying*

MARCUS McHENRY, *his unstable younger brother*

MARTHA McHENRY, *their mother*

FELICITY SPELLMAN, *Marcus's girlfriend*

ARTHUR McLOUGHLIN, *a neighbour*

FATHER ANTHONY O'DRISCOLL, *a family friend*

The play takes place in the late 1990s in a fashionable Dublin suburb

ACT ONE

Scene One

We are in a spacious, high-ceilinged bedroom with a large closed window in the centre that looks out on a fire-escape and the garden beneath, framing a view of tree-tops – leafy because it is high summer – and the great grey-blue sky above and beyond everything.

JORDAN *is lying propped on several pillows in his bed at the right of the room. A bald, bare-chested man of about thirty, he's been through chemotherapy and the knife often enough to look like it, although at this point he remains more agile and articulate than he'll be in the last stages of sickness. A small TV sits on a night-table beside the bed, but it's only on in the small hours with the volume down, when its flicker comforts the darkness. A plastic bib for* JORDAN*'s liquid suppers hangs from its rabbit ears.*

There is a religious image – modern and primitive at the same time – on the wall beside the window, preferably the popular Christ of Evie Hone.

MARCUS, *a year or so younger than his dying brother, is seated in a fold-up wheelchair as if reading to* JORDAN *from a paperback. Bookshelves fill out the wall behind him on either side of the bedroom door. In the middle of the room we see an antique hostess trolley full of medicine bottles, syringes, syrups, towels, water carafes, the blister foils of analgesics and a large red hairdryer.*

MARCUS (*rapidly*). At the first sad stroke of the Angelus from the tower of the parish church, they kneeled together, the two of them, in heartfelt, heaving prayer. But the saltwater scent of her sex and the earthen warmth of her ass demented Father Cornelius. He ripped the flimsy chemise from the brown of her breast as she whimpered in gratitude. Then he tore the burgundy, no, the *lavender* suspenders from her moist, child-bearing hips so that she lay divested beneath him on the altar. Like a saint's ascension in a sentimental painting, the whites of her eyes rotated in ecstasy under the powdered stardust on her eyelids; (*To himself.*) but that's boring. Who gives a shit about her eyelids? And we skip accordingly with the fingers of one hand as far as . . . Her pleasure was peaking already. He could smell it.

'No-one has ever given me a multiple orgasm,' she said. 'Not even Father Abbot. May I call you My Lord?' 'You may call me Monsignor,' he said. 'It's in the bag. The bishop said so.' He elongated subtly inside her as her pastel-pink artificial nails dragged scarlet scratchmarks across his . . . youthful buttocks.

JORDAN. His masculine haunches.

MARCUS. The precise and powerful thrusts of his masculine haunches. Better. 'There's a pimple somewhere there,' he said. 'You need to watch that.' Tears of appreciation filled her eyes as his seed sprouted.

JORDAN. Spouted.

MARCUS. Spouted. (*Pause.*) That's a very Viennese slip of the tongue. Perhaps I *should* go into psychoanalysis. (*Pause.*) What were we calling this woman?

JORDAN. We didn't give her a name.

MARCUS. The nameless, shameless woman smelled his scalp and the brown hair under his left axilla.

JORDAN. I prefer armpit.

MARCUS. He was filling her with more genetic material than ever before. In the midst of that seminal event lay so much delightful DNA –

JORDAN. Fuck off. *I'm* the fourth-year medical student. Or was.

MARCUS. From the which it should be possible –

JORDAN. Might be possible –

MARCUS. Must be possible, at some point in the foreseeable future, to establish precisely why it is that one person should be born with an incorrigible psychiatric condition which fucks up just about everyone and everything, and another person be born with a tiny terminal disease already evolving within him, whose adult conduct of his daily life is always and everywhere . . . dignified.

JORDAN. I'll never have an erection if you don't stop digressing.

MARCUS. Her boobs were buoyant. She had put on fake tan all over, but it left a ghost bikini. 'My Sally Gap belongs to you,' she said. 'My Furry Glen is your personal playground.'.

Enter their MOTHER *in a characteristically brisk and busy manner. She crosses the room, throws the window wide to let in air, picks an aerosol canister from the hostess trolley and freshens the place in short bursts. She continues tidying as* MARCUS *goes on narrating. He has segued from one discourse to another as she came in.*

MARCUS. This was one of multiple mystical moments experienced by Father Cornelius. He's fully persuaded that the stigmatist will become a saint in the fullness of time. Hundreds of people are already being canonised yearly by the present Holy Father, and the only requirement appears, in the absence of any married candidates, to be an active hex on sex in order to achieve the state of holiness, alongside utter ignorance of the way in which ordinary human beings live and die in the dirty, fertile world that God looked at and thought was a good thing.

The MOTHER *peels the duvet off* JORDAN *without consulting him and removes its cover to replace it with a clean one.* JORDAN *is wearing only tight pyjama bottoms. His thighs grip a plastic beaker that collects his urine.*

JORDAN. Who's coming?

MOTHER. Anthony, love.

JORDAN. Ah.

MOTHER. Is that all right?

JORDAN. Of course. He's very good.

MOTHER. He's bringing Holy Communion.

JORDAN. Ah.

MARCUS. Hasn't Father Anthony some for me as well?
Nobody thinks about Marcus the Dark Horse.

MOTHER (*to* MARCUS, *angrily*). I may be a knave but I'm
not a fool. I'm long enough on the earth to have done things
that aren't heavenly, but I'm not a fool. (*To* JORDAN.) Do
you need to be cooled? Shall I blow on you?

JORDAN *bobs his head. The* MOTHER *kneels and begins
to blow – slowly, smoothly, sensuously – on her son's ruined
face and his bare chest to cool him.*

That nice? Hmm?

JORDAN. Umm.

MOTHER. What am I wearing?

JORDAN. Blue.

MOTHER. God, you're a silly-billy.

MARCUS (*head cocked*). Did I hear a Ballyshannon accent or
did I not?

MOTHER (*to* JORDAN). What *perfume* am I wearing?

JORDAN. A nice one.

MOTHER. The one you bought me in London two years ago.

JORDAN. Ah.

MOTHER. That one.

MARCUS. I did hear a Ballyshannon accent.

MOTHER. There's nothing wrong with your sense of smell.
It's just the pollen count.

MARCUS. And you haven't been next or near your native
place for thirty-two years. Tell me this, though, truthfully.
Was it before or during or after your stint as a Vincent's

nurse in search of a surgical registrar with the right potential that you started to speak like the houses on Wellington Road?

MOTHER (*to* MARCUS). It was on the train coming up. (*To* JORDAN.) What would you say to six or seven seedless grapes and a spoon of ice-cream? I took the skin off too before I crushed them. The thing is to swallow very slowly. Hmm?

JORDAN. Umm.

MOTHER. Lovely and cool when it slides down.

JORDAN. Umm.

The MOTHER *puts a clean pyjama top on* JORDAN, *sprinkles him with eau-de-toilette, straightens the duvet and leaves. As she passes* MARCUS:

MOTHER. Just take your tablets and empty the dishwasher.

As she closes the door behind her, MARCUS *nips across to his brother's bed and bends over him.*

MARCUS. Speaking of odours. Of what or whom am I reeking right now?

JORDAN. I don't know. I've lost it, Marcus. My sense of smell.

MARCUS. A crossword clue. Better by far than the Body of Christ.

JORDAN. Morphine.

MARCUS. A woman's body.

JORDAN. First taste; then smell. What next?

MARCUS. It's hay fucking fever. That's all. You need an antihistamine.

JORDAN. It's the tumour. Growing again. I need a miracle. (*Pause.*) I *can* smell something. It's not me, is it?

MARCUS (*gravely*). It is the state of Felicity.

JORDAN. I thought I did. Is it me?

MARCUS. Felicity. She sat on my lap last night for a full two hours. I was stiff afterwards. And I haven't changed my clothes since. I like her whiff.

JORDAN. Alarm bells? Wedding bells?

MARCUS. Say: chimes. It's a complex process. It begins with holding hands and it ends with the girlfriend buying your underwear in Dunnes Stores. In between, of course, there are ages and stages. First the kiss, and then the French kiss. At day five to six, she sits on your lap. Seven to eight, she sits side-saddle while you rummage her breasts, and she fakes those moaning sounds that can't be real because women's boobs don't have that many nerve-ends.

JORDAN. They do. I was breastfed. I remember distinctly. You don't, because you weren't. It explains everything. That's why you're an ass man.

MARCUS (*intent upon his theme*). But the boobs are only another decoy. Now it's week two, and it's almost a relationship. Time to play with her beautiful bum. More moaning and groaning as she sits astride you and you're just about to tell her the private pet-name for your penis, but the tour of her sacred places hasn't ended yet and there's one remaining sanctuary more precious than the grotto at Lourdes that you haven't seen and you're not about to, because she's . . . thinking. (*As in 'tick tock'*.) Think, think.

JORDAN. Think what?

MARCUS. She's thinking: are there redheads in his family? I couldn't bear a redheaded child. She's thinking: where has he been for the last five years? Has he been in prison? We could never go to the States then. Has he been in religious life? Is he going to go to prison for that? Why is he doing a Master's in Philosophy at this stage of his life when his classmates in that fee-paying school of his are traipsing through the Bar Library and the teaching hospitals, chartering helicopters to fly to their holiday homes at the weekend? (*Pause.*) If the brother goes, he'll inherit everything. The leafy silence of those wealthy streets. But the mother's young enough. Could I live with a damaging and dysfunctional woman for the first twenty-five years of my married life? (*Pause.*) She thinks.

MARCUS *sits on the floor, leaning his back against the bed.*

JORDAN. You're very hard on Mum.

MARCUS. Of course, all I need do to reassure her is to tell her the truth. Your fears are groundless, I could say. Priests, prisons, contraband. I was committed to something much more important. I was committed to the closed ward of a psychiatric hospital for two years. I was electrocuted thirty times. Now I am earthed. Every antidepressant in creation has passed through my penis into the toilet bowl. And I owe it all to Doctor Betty O'Gara from Borris-in-Ossory and to a stone called lithium which has many uses. It primes the firing pins of nuclear bombs and it makes mental patients sufficiently clear-headed to appreciate for the first time the ruin they have caused and cannot undo in other people's lives. End of story.

JORDAN. Finished?

MARCUS. Finished.

JORDAN. You're very hard on Mum. I was saying.

MARCUS. You think.

JORDAN. She suffers more than you do. More than I do.

MARCUS. I've noticed.

JORDAN. She suffered when Dad died. A sudden death is more terrible for those who are left behind.

MARCUS. You sound like the brochures in the church porch.

JORDAN. Yet to watch the suffering of someone we love can be worse. I read that in the *Reader's Digest*. Or perhaps it was the *Sacred Heart Messenger*.

MARCUS. You didn't?

JORDAN. They're easy to hold if your hand is shaky.

MARCUS. But the print is tiny.

JORDAN. I can do a page. A page and a half. Then it's like the TV when it snows. Swirls of colour. Whiteness. (*Pause.*) Do my eyes.

MARCUS. I don't want to do your eyes.

JORDAN. Why?

MARCUS. Because when I do your eyes, you look as if you're crying. It's sheer manipulation.

JORDAN. We shall rise again.

MARCUS. No, we won't. We won't rise again. Jesus of Nazareth stood at my bedside one night in the hospital, in the small hours, and he told me that he promised eternal life to those who believed, and not immortal life to those who behaved, and that the meaning of what he had said got lost in its passage from Aramaic to Greek. And he apologised.

JORDAN. What did you say?

MARCUS. I said nothing. I had nothing to say. That was how I knew it was a true vision. I offered him a major tranquilliser from a store I'd been hiding in my slippers toward a suicide bid; but he kissed the palms of my hands and he disappeared.

MARCUS *gets up, kisses the palms of his brother's hands, lays them back on the bed, and fetches eye-drops from the hostess trolley. He applies them very precisely as his brother stares up at him. This is something they do often.*

Up at the ceiling. Good. (*Pause.*) What do you really think?

JORDAN. The tumour is pressing on the optic nerve.

MARCUS. And?

JORDAN. You're very hard on Mum.

MARCUS. What has she to do with your optic nerve?

JORDAN. I was thinking of how a cancer grows. Beautiful, really; but lethal. Do the other eye more.

MARCUS. Listen, you shit. I love you. I love you as if you were a woman. If you were a woman, I'd marry you. But you mustn't think that, because you're dying, you alone have total insight into the human condition. That's how the chaplains go on, and it's boring.

A shout from the garden as ARTHUR *approaches. A benign Methodist businessman and, in the absence of his own expatriate son, an adoptive uncle to the two brothers who are his next-door neighbours, his social ebullience almost conceals fracture and hurt.*

ARTHUR. Ahoy there. Permission to come alongside.

MARCUS. It's Captain Haddock.

JORDAN (*unable to project the greeting*). Arthur!

ARTHUR. Coming alongside anyway.

JORDAN. Empty my thing.

MARCUS *retrieves the beaker from beneath the duvet.*

MARCUS. Not only filled but fulfilled.

JORDAN. I was pissing all the time you were talking. (*Pause.*) I would like to meet her.

MARCUS. Who?

JORDAN. Felicity. I would like to meet her.

ARTHUR (*at the window, kindly and comical*). Permission to come aboard.

JORDAN. Granted and given.

ARTHUR (*climbs elaborately in*). That fire-escape will be the death of me.

MARCUS. It's the life and soul of you, Arthur. It's the best form of exercise you get.

ARTHUR. You should sail with me. Like your brother does. Then you'd see.

JORDAN. So. Any dispatches?

ARTHUR. Dispatches galore. Number 123 was withdrawn at £927,000. Proper order too. It has a hallway you could sell to a four-star hotel.

JORDAN. One twenty three.

ARTHUR. Eighteen granite steps to the boot-scrapers. Same as one twenty seven.

JORDAN. One twenty three was the child with cerebral palsy. And the father committed suicide.

ARTHUR. Well, you don't put that in the brochure. (*Pause.*) Almost a million. Mind you, isn't there an embassy two doors down, admittedly only an African one, but still; and the chestnuts in the front garden must have been planted in the age of the tall ships. Sure they're tall ships themselves. If you stand in among those chestnuts –

MARCUS. Where the security man used to urinate on guard duty. You'd hear the patter on the ivy.

ARTHUR. – on a day with a force four south-westerly breeze, you could close your eyes and be twenty miles out circling the Kish. It's Heaven. If they say that Heaven's any better, they're selling you a pup.

JORDAN. What else?

ARTHUR. A communication from the plains of Alberta. Rodney, my only beloved is well, I think. 'Good' might be pushing it. He still does the hot-air ballooning. And he still shoots the woodpeckers. Of course, a trial separation is, I suppose, what it says it is. A trial. A tribulation. He misses the boys. Misses the house. Misses Pamela. Misses not being able to punch that Serbian fellow in the face. In the old days, you could punch a chap if he looked at your missus. Now, if he sleeps with her, you have to invite him over to a mediation workshop.

MARCUS (*emptying the beaker out the window*). Do you know, Jordan, your waters are annihilating the rhododendron? What are the specialists prescribing?

ARTHUR. It's the children, really. The two of them are the living image of . . . *moi*, God help us. Look at their picture, you'd want to weep. So I went out this morning and I did the block with my camera and tripod. Must have taken a hundred shots of the neighbourhood; and the great thing was, I could stand into all of them myself with that thirty second timer thing. It means their sense of themselves, of their heritage, will anchor them when they're at sea. I think they'll find it fascinating. All Pamela can show them is coconut trees and natives wearing Honolulu garlands; and that bastard of a Serb, excuse me.

JORDAN. Please God –

MARCUS. Please goodness –

JORDAN. Please goodness everything will work out for them soon.

ARTHUR. The door of hope must never be closed.

MARCUS. The door of hope must always be closed. Hope is an erection without an ejaculation. It hurts to hope. (MARCUS *closes the window and slips the beaker back into the bed.*) Wouldn't it be interesting, though, to compare the PH of the urine of two brothers on radically different yet complementary regimes, and then decide which prescription would destroy a prize-winning garden more rapidly?

ARTHUR. You're a terrible man. Do you know that?

MARCUS. Would it destroy your cannabis? It's taking over the greenhouse.

ARTHUR. Listen. You'll destroy my reputation. (*To* JORDAN.) If Rodney hadn't planted them, I'd have pulled them out years ago. They're just a connection with him, is all. Remind me what a rogue he was. A bit like the watch. (*Shows it.*) The Islamic numerals, see, from when he was in Riyadh, working. People think I'm pro-Arab when they see it, but I'm not. I hate them.

MARCUS. I hate everybody, except my mother whom I abominate. Jordan, on the other hand, loves the Creation. Years of uninterrupted vomiting have made him a mystic.

ARTHUR. Watch reminds me. I brought this. (*Rummages in his pocket, produces a stopwatch.*) For you, Jordan. Our . . . stopwatch. (*Holds it up.*) Now. I want you to keep this close. (*Winds it.*) Its tick is very quiet, very consoling. (*Listens.*) I'm going to put it in under your pillow so that, every time you see it or hear it, (*Passes it to* JORDAN *who examines it close up.*) you are to think of the Commodore's race this time next year, with a whole flotilla of Dragons out in the Bay, and yourself steering, not crewing, skippering, and a beautiful woman – no, a pretty girl, much safer – waiting for you, out there on the terrace of the club, watching our victory through binoculars. Dah dah. (*Takes it back from* JORDAN.)

JORDAN. Dah dah.

ARTHUR. Life, as the man said, is not plain sailing; but plain sailing is the best part of life.

MARCUS. That's an epigram, Arthur. Well done.

ARTHUR. Thank you. It just came to me. (*Lifts the pillow to place the stopwatch down. Finds other items.*) I beg your pardon. I didn't know.

JORDAN. The relics. Mum has great faith.

MARCUS (*in a servile brogue*). She do, fadder. She do.

JORDAN. I wish that one of us did. She is so outnumbered.

MARCUS. Take your pick, Arthur. The dead plant is a palm blessed by a Dominican Prior, no less, on Palm Sunday. They have the power. Even a Methodist would know about palms.

ARTHUR. And, if he did, he wouldn't laugh.

MARCUS. The dirty looking cellophane pouch is dust from the catacombs; or is it Jerusalem?

JORDAN. Jerusalem. Jerusalem next year!

MARCUS. And the tiny bit of cloth, yes, is a fragment from a habit that was worn in the convent by The Little Flower. From a collector's point of view, it is worth a fortune. It's like the Cape of Good Hope Triangular.

ARTHUR (*awkward*). Well, I suppose the stopwatch is a bit of a relic too.

MARCUS. My mother has always confused the supernatural with the paranormal. Her faith is simply beyond belief. And yet there was a time in my childhood when she'd take us by the hand and walk out of Sunday mass if she didn't like the politics of the homily.

Door opens. MOTHER *enters with a J-cloth in one hand and dessert bowl in the other.*

MOTHER. Arthur McLoughlin.

ARTHUR. Martha McHenry. I hope you don't mind.

MOTHER. Mind? Why would I mind? (*She crosses the room to open the window again.*)

ARTHUR. And you heard about Number 123? Withdrawn at nine twenty seven K.

MOTHER (*she has begun her habitual spraying and wiping*). It should have gone for more than a million. Number 169 fetched £800,000 twelve months ago and the basement is dark.

JORDAN. Number 169 is where the gay couple lived. He should have been charged with manslaughter and not with murder. It was a crime of the heart.

MOTHER (*to* MARCUS). That's what happens when you do something that puts you beyond the protection of your class. For ever.

MARCUS (*to* ARTHUR). 'Don't call me gay,' he said. 'I'm gloomy. Call me queer. At least queer has a certain ring to it.'

MOTHER (*holding the bowl, to* JORDAN). Would you like it now or after Holy Communion?

JORDAN. What do you think?

MOTHER. Doesn't make a blind bit of difference.

JORDAN. Later.

MOTHER. The re-runs of *Kojak* start on Wednesday.

JORDAN. They don't?

MOTHER. They do.

ARTHUR. The bald fellow? (*Aware of the gaffe.*) Rodney was mad on *Wonder Woman*.

MOTHER (*to* ARTHUR). Jordan used to watch *Kojak* with his dad.

MARCUS. Ditto.

MOTHER. His dad used to fall asleep beside him. Jordan would hold his hand while he slept.

MARCUS (*pause. To* ARTHUR). Then Kojak would solve the case and the two of them would climb the long, weary stairs to bed. Like Pooh Bear and Christopher Robin. The father and the son. Amen.

MOTHER (*reluctantly*). That's right. He remembers too.

MARCUS. Do you know what I remember? I remember when I was seven. I was looking through the porthole of the operating room and I saw him there in the theatre in his green gown. Somebody was open on the table, and he was standing under the lights, sweating blood, with the dark outline of his mouth like a zero on the face-mask, and the scrub nurse was wiping his forehead slowly, slowly with a white cloth while he worked, and the whole team was waiting around him with their gloved hands held up, and I realised suddenly that I was watching the Last Supper, and that my father was God, and my life would be a failure.

MOTHER. There was no porthole in the door of the operating theatre.

MARCUS. There was something I could see through. It was only a moment, but I could.

Distant front door bell.

MOTHER. That's Anthony. That's Father Anthony, Arthur. He'll want to meet you. He thinks the world of Methodists.

In fact, he thinks the world of Protestants and Orthodox Russians and Jews and Mohammedans and Buddhists. Never forget the Buddhists. The only people he can't stand are his own religious superiors and, of course, the Pope.

She leaves. There is a moment's silence.

MARCUS. There was a porthole.

JORDAN. I remember.

ARTHUR. I was in that hospital myself. But you don't notice detail when you're passing kidney stones.

JORDAN. When you're dying, you see everything. It's like hang-gliding over Venice. The streets are redeemed as canals and the houses are rooted in water.

ARTHUR (*jovially*). How would you know?

JORDAN (*to* MARCUS). Don't be rude to Anthony.

MARCUS. I wasn't rude. I was . . . robust.

JORDAN. You were a nasty little shit.

MARCUS. Not little. I thought he was a Jesuit. Because of the way he shook hands. And his irony. That's why. Then I found out he's only a Holy Ghost.

ARTHUR. Great men. Great rugby tradition.

MARCUS. The Holy Ghost doesn't play rugby. The Holy Ghost plays . . . wind instruments.

Door opens. MOTHER *enters with the priest, a man in his mid-forties who is wearing clerical dress and a roman collar.*

MOTHER. Now. Here we are. Father Anthony O'Driscoll. Mr. Arthur McLoughlin, our next-door neighbour.

MARCUS. Where the nanny from Connemara had her baby in the hot press in 1962.

ARTHUR. Before my time, need I say.

He and the priest shake hands.

MOTHER. Father Anthony is back from Rwanda. Arthur is a Methodist.

ARTHUR. Pavilion member.

MARCUS. Arthur, in the absence of an available Presbyterian or Jew, you are very important to our family's sense of social ecumenism at the millennium.

FATHER ANTHONY (*to* MARCUS). The philosopher. I'm still thinking about what you said.

MARCUS. What did I say, Tony?

FATHER ANTHONY. What didn't you say is more like it. I was . . . enthralled.

MARCUS. Tony, I apologise. I thought you were a Jesuit. I have nothing against the Holy Ghost. The thing is, I was interviewed for the Jesuit noviciate when I was manic. Of course, they threw me out. One of them asked me: 'In Biblical language, in a scriptural idiom, do you believe that you are being guided by the Holy Spirit of the God of Jesus?'

I said to them: 'I am the Holy Spirit.' (*Wistfully.*) And I was.

MOTHER. Mad as a hatter.

MARCUS. Not mad. Madness is great fun. I was mentally ill. That's altogether different.

MOTHER (*fiercely*). You can't stop talking about yourself. You'll be sick until you stop talking about yourself. (*To the others.*) I'm sorry.

MARCUS. Family life is not a family show, padre.

MOTHER. And look at our patient: the most patient patient in the world.

JORDAN. I love the gear, Anthony. The dog collar's cool.

FATHER ANTHONY. Simple arithmetic. The washing machine's kaput. Now, if you wear a shirt, you change it every day. Well, every second day. On the other hand, you get a week out of the sackcloth and ashes, and nobody notices the dirt.

MARCUS. I would have thought the dirt on the Roman collar had never been so noticeable.

FATHER ANTHONY. It's a fair point.

MOTHER. A lot of it is the tabloids.

MARCUS. A lot of it is the broadsheets.

FATHER ANTHONY. A lot of it is the truth.

ARTHUR. How can you know that, Father?

FATHER ANTHONY. Because the truth always makes you feel ill. (*Pause.*) But the thing is, about this. (*He touches his collar.*) I'd rather be jostled in the street than fawned over at a cocktail party. It feels more . . . loyal.

ARTHUR. Anyhow, it's better than Rwanda.

FATHER ANTHONY. In some ways.

ARTHUR. Rwanda. The heart of darkness.

MARCUS. Arthur. In re. Rwanda. Refresh my memory. Who are the goodies: the Hutus or the Tutsis? Who are the baddies: the Tutsis or the Hutus?

ARTHUR (*embarrassed*). Couldn't say, I'm afraid. Better on the Serbs.

MARCUS. My point is –

MOTHER. Never mind, Arthur. He thinks I'm stupid too. I'll leave you all to your theological college. I have cleaning to do, and cooking, and ironing, and accounting. (*To* MARCUS.) I have lots of occupational therapy for you downstairs, Marcus. I'll give you a gong. Come when I call.

She leaves, closing the door behind her.

JORDAN. So. See how these Christians love one another.

ARTHUR. I remember now. About the Hutus.

MARCUS (*to* FATHER ANTHONY). I adore my mother. She squeezed me out into the world. For that alone I can forgive her nothing.

FATHER ANTHONY. She's under tremendous pressure.

MARCUS. I was under tremendous pressure for two years. In hospital. She never once visited me.

JORDAN. Not true. She stood outside the revolving doors on four occasions. On the fourth and final attempt, she sent up a dressing-gown.

ARTHUR. I think I might safely slip away at this point.

FATHER ANTHONY (*to* MARCUS). You must have been very sick. Two years is –

MARCUS. Two Christmases. Carbonised turkey with plastic cutlery. And a paper hat. I may not believe in Silent Night, but I still believe in Santa.

FATHER ANTHONY. I'm sure you still believe in your mother too.

MARCUS. I adore my mum. I had my first erection rubbing sun-oil on the back of her legs out there in the garden under the honeysuckle, I was twelve, which is pretty good going, I would have thought. I ran away to look at it in the mirror in her bedroom.

FATHER ANTHONY. Sure that's perfectly natural.

ARTHUR. Intoxicating, this, but too heady for a Methodist, I'm afraid. God bless, good health, and goodbye. To be continued!

And he leaves as he came, by the fire escape.

FATHER ANTHONY. Right.

MARCUS. Wrong.

FATHER ANTHONY. Look. What I mean is . . . We're very strange creatures, you know. But our strangeness, the strangest part of us, is the place where meaning emerges, or, to put it in God-talk, it's the place where the Lord seeks shelter within us. It's the shed of Bethlehem in the world of Caesar. So we must cherish our . . . difficult strangeness because it is the venue of Yahweh. It is the tent of meeting. Do you know?

MARCUS. I couldn't have put it better myself.

FATHER ANTHONY. What I mean is . . . Take me. I entered
the Order because I loved the sense of community, of course,
and the prestige of ministry, probably, and the manliness
of the missions, yes, that too, and because I wanted to serve
something larger than my own ego; but also because I was
afraid and I was hiding from myself. (*Pause.*) But the thing
is, you see, God . . . God kisses our weaknesses and trans-
forms them into strengths. That's what we mean by grace,
isn't it? When God breathes life into our existence. Like my
mother. I had whooping cough when I was only a few days
old, and she breathed her breath into my mouth and my nose
for three days without once sleeping or resting. (*Pause;
distant ringing of gong; he becomes self-conscious.*) Anyhow. I'd better give you Holy Communion and go. I have
to return the community car by four.

He takes the pyx out of his pocket and opens it.

MARCUS. Should I leave?

FATHER ANTHONY. Don't be silly. Do you want to receive?

MARCUS. I believe . . . not. My psychiatrist tells me that, if
I find myself thinking about God, she'll increase the dosage
to inhibit obsessional ruminations.

FATHER ANTHONY (*opens the pyx, removes a host*). Jordan,
this is Jesus the Christ, the Lamb of God, who takes away
all the pain and imperfection of our world.

JORDAN. Lord, I am not worthy to receive you. Only say the
word and I shall be healed. (*Distant gong again.*)

FATHER ANTHONY. The body and the blood of Christ. The
body broken for us; the blood poured out for us.

JORDAN. That's too large.

FATHER ANTHONY. What is?

JORDAN. The host.

MARCUS. What he means, Anthony, is that the old plasticky
wafer goes down easily but the new bready one makes him
gag. He's losing the ability to swallow.

FATHER ANTHONY (*he breaks the host in two*). O.K?

JORDAN. Still too big.

> *Gong in the distance. The priest breaks the bread again and again. He sits a tiny fraction on* JORDAN's *tongue.*

JORDAN. Thank you. (*He blesses himself slowly.*) Amen.

FATHER ANTHONY. Marcus?

MARCUS. You really believe?

FATHER ANTHONY. Where else would I go? He has the words of eternal life. Do you want? (*He holds up part of a host.*)

MARCUS. I meant what I said. Belief in God is a prime symptom of my illness.

FATHER ANTHONY (*to* JORDAN). Will you give me holy communion? (*Hands the host to him.*)

JORDAN. Body of Christ.

FATHER ANTHONY. Amen.

MARCUS. Dr. Betty O'Gara says to me: 'Are you feeling close to God today?' If I say no, they give me back my clothes and let me walk around the grounds without a male nurse. If I say yes, I get more shock treatment.

JORDAN. Swallowed. (*Fervently.*) Thanks be to God.

MARCUS. It's why I envy Jordan. His suffering is so male, so reputable. Mine is unwholesome. He can show his sutures and everybody's eyes fill up. When I show them my arm, they wince and shrink away. Come see. Go tell.

> *He rolls up the sleeve of his shirt to reveal dreadful scar wounds on the inside of his wrist.*

FATHER ANTHONY. Jesus Christ. (*He comes closer.*) Why didn't you just take sleeping pills?

MARCUS. I did. My mother's Mogadon. Her Zimovane. Her tranks. My Melloril. Other associated anxyllitics. Tri-cyclics too: Anafranil, Prothiadine, Zispin, Parstellan.

In the ambulance, in the hospital, my mother didn't want me to be revived. She said: 'Let him die in peace for once and for all.'

JORDAN. She thought he'd be brain dead. She thought he'd be a vegetable or a mineral.

MARCUS. But Jordan made them work on me. The SHO's, the registrar, the consultant himself.

JORDAN. I gave you mouth-to-mouth in the Casualty. They pulled me off you. I said: 'Bring him back.' There was a little girl, with her teeth hanging out of her mouth from a blow or an accident. She kept watching you. She was your guardian angel. (*Pause.*) After two days –

MARCUS. Not three, I'm afraid, Anthony. Would have been nice. Would have been biblical.

JORDAN. Two nights, two days.

MARCUS. I woke up and I wept because I was still alive in the world.

Bedroom bursts open and MOTHER *enters. She carries a small gong and beater that she starts to drum in a frenzy close to* MARCUS's *face.*

MOTHER (*to* MARCUS). Why didn't you answer? Why won't you? Are you always mocking me? Do you need to treat me like afterbirth? Are you still talking about your ludicrous little illness? Or you are talking about women again? There isn't a woman in the whole of your community who'd walk down Grafton Street with you. Why do you think about them all the time? Maybe you should think about them going to the toilet, going Uuhh, Uuhh, Uuhh in the toilet? Maybe that would quieten you about women?

MARCUS. Maybe it would excite me.

The MOTHER *strikes* MARCUS *violently across the face. Blackout.*

Scene Two

Setting as before. Two weeks later. It's almost noon on a warm summer's day. The windows are wide open.

The MOTHER *is sitting on* JORDAN's *bed, shaving her leg with a battery razor. He is wearing a large plastic bib. His condition has deteriorated.*

MOTHER (*humming for a time*). Well. Am I pretty?

JORDAN. Very.

MOTHER. If you don't give me any more grief over Neapolitan ice-cream, I'll wear the mauve dress for you tomorrow.

JORDAN. The mauve dress was . . . Connemara.

MOTHER. The mauve dress was Paris. I'm the only one in our family with a memory.

JORDAN. Do you remember me with hair?

MOTHER (*upset*). Don't be saying things like that. Of course I do.

JORDAN. I don't.

MOTHER. You'll have it again. I'll be nagging you to go get it cut.

JORDAN. Do you remember Marcus when he was himself?

MOTHER (*she finishes shaving her leg and looks at* JORDAN's *cheek*). I'll do you while I'm at it. (*And she begins to do so.*)

JORDAN. Do you?

MOTHER. Do I what?

ARTHUR *hails from the garden.*

ARTHUR. Anybody aboard?

MOTHER. That bloody man. (*Calls.*) Yes, Arthur?

JORDAN. Mum?

MOTHER. What is it, chick?

JORDAN. I love him in Christ. Pretend I'm asleep.

MOTHER (*removing* JORDAN*'s plastic bib and calling out at the same time*). Arthur!

ARTHUR. *Voilà.* (*Steps into the room from the fire escape.*) How's my friend?

MOTHER. Sleeping. We'll go downstairs.

ARTHUR. You stay where you are, Martha. I'll slip away. (*Pause.*) I'm afraid the news back from the advertising people wasn't great.

MOTHER. It was very kind of you to try.

ARTHUR. The problem was . . . not so much the psychiatry in and of itself. Anybody can be astray in themselves. I sometimes think I'm potty too. And it wasn't his age profile either. So maybe it was the whole . . . concatenation, if you will. Not just the hospital but the hole in the CV as well. Do you know? Then again, the door of hope must always be kept open.

MOTHER. A Master's in Philosophy. What in God's name are you good for, after a Master's in Philosophy?

ARTHUR. A . . . Doctorate in Philosophy?

MOTHER. Could Marcus be an auctioneer? All you need to be an auctioneer is neck.

ARTHUR. Neck could be an advantage at times. I wish I had some neck.

MOTHER. Or could he be a quantity surveyor? If people knew he was a manic depressive, they'd forgive him for only being a quantity surveyor.

ARTHUR. You know, if he weren't to be so . . . frank and forthright sometimes, then I think Marcus would make a wonderful teacher.

MOTHER. Do you mean a secondary teacher?

ARTHUR. Why not?

MOTHER. Arthur, when did you last see a secondary teacher in a club in Stephen's Green?

ARTHUR. Point.

MOTHER. On the other hand, the clubs are full of auctioneers. They wear braces and bifocal spectacles to look like barristers.

ARTHUR. I can see why they've taken over the place, at two per cent. I only ever got two per cent in a Latin exam.

MOTHER. I blame his religion teachers. Not the priests. The priests knew what was what. The priests knew they were training a professional class to take over the administration of the culture when their fathers retired. So it was one religion class per week and one maths class per day with a double period on a Friday. No, it was lay people with beards and banjos who did all the damage. I remember them well. They filled his head with all kinds of nonsense about solidarity and brotherhood and humpback whales and God only knows what else. (*Pause.*) What Marcus can't understand, and never understood, is that you can fall out of grace, you can fall out of pride, you can fall out of favour with God himself, but you can't fall out of your social class. If you fall out of your social class, there is no way back. You are doomed. Because the only things your community values are power, profit, and prestige. That is the gospel truth.

ARTHUR. Amen, I'm afraid.

MOTHER. It's not enough to do good. You have to do well.

ARTHUR. I said it to Rodney a thousand times. And what does he do? Clears out of the country. I thought he'd got some girl into trouble. No, he was just footloose. Well, now he's footsore.

MOTHER. I knew it as a girl in Ballyshannon. I targeted Jordan's father, God forgive me. The only child of a wealthy

couple. There was an echo in every room in that house.
Twenty-five feet from the fireplace fender to the beautiful
walnut door. Amn't I paying for it now?

JORDAN. Mum.

MOTHER. Jesus, Mary and Joseph, I forgot.

JORDAN. Hmm?

MOTHER. I didn't mean that.

JORDAN. What? (*Pause.*) What didn't you mean?

MOTHER. I don't know.

JORDAN (*pause*). I was asleep. I'm sorry. (*Calls.*) Arthur!

ARTHUR. How's my skipper then?

JORDAN. Navigating. But without charts.

ARTHUR. Next year, next summer, next midsummer day,
we'll be under sail off Arklow. And we'll navigate by
starlight. Cassiopeia. Orion. Polaris. The Plough. What do
you say?

JORDAN. And Marcus.

ARTHUR. And Marcus, by God. And your mother.

MOTHER. With my vertigo? Go way out of that. I even got
seasick at the Boat Shows.

Knock – a Beethoven's Fifth – on the door. It opens and
MARCUS *steps into the room. He has papers and*
magazines under his arm.

JORDAN. Speak of the devil.

ARTHUR. Young man.

MARCUS. Old man.

ARTHUR. Wimbledon weather.

MARCUS. Fastnet weather.

ARTHUR. Absolutely.

MARCUS. How's the cannabis?

ARTHUR. Tall as triffids.

MOTHER (*to* MARCUS). Where were you?

MARCUS. I was starting the dishwasher.

MOTHER. It was only half full. Have you no sense?

MARCUS. Not according to Doctor Betty O'Gara; and I have that in writing. (*Pause.*) What time is the mass? I want to ring the bell. I want to ring the gong.

MOTHER. Anthony should be here in a few minutes.

MARCUS. If he isn't, I'll say it myself. (*Points at* ARTHUR.) Is that heretic coming?

MOTHER. You're the heretic.

ARTHUR. I am the mandatory Protestant, and very pleased to be.

JORDAN. Is Felicity here?

MARCUS. She's coming with Anthony. Tony could do with a bit of Felicity in his life.

MOTHER. Does he even know the girl?

MARCUS. No. But I'm sure he'll love her just as much as you do.

MOTHER. You haven't sent him out of his way?

MARCUS. She's round the corner from him. I made sure she lived in the best area before I slept with her.

MOTHER. Have you no decorum? The mass is being said in this room today.

MARCUS. In deference to the Ancient Mariner among us, I think we ought to speak instead of a Eucharist or a service of Holy Communion.

ARTHUR. Jordan has shown me a head and shoulders snapshot of Felicity in the bandstand on the pier, and, if the Ancient Mariner may say so, I think I would call her a most womanly woman. When I meet a person, I like to know whether they're male or female. In Felicity's case, there is no room for doubt. She is a daughter of Eve.

MARCUS. I know what you mean, Arthur. She has great boobs.

MOTHER. Marcus.

JORDAN. Nineteenth-century bosom, twentieth-century legs, and a smile for the coming millennium.

ARTHUR. I wish I could say things just like that, off the top of my head. Do you have to be a Catholic?

MOTHER. I shall leave the lot of you to your forensic examination of this poor unfortunate girl. If she only knew. (*She gets up to leave.*)

ARTHUR. And I shall go smarten myself up for Father Anthony. (*Pause; turns.*) Forgive my ignorance, but will he come supplied?

MOTHER. Supplied with what?

JORDAN. The bread of life and the cup of eternal salvation.

ARTHUR. Precisely. We Methodists use fruit-juice, as it happens, but I have a rather nice bottle of claret which it would be a great privilege to serve at this Lord's Supper.

MARCUS. Bring it.

MOTHER. Anthony will have what he needs.

MARCUS. Perhaps. But does he have what he wants?

ARTHUR. Well . . . to be continued.

He leaves by the fire escape, the MOTHER by the door.

MARCUS (*chucks the magazines in the wheelchair and stands at the window, looking out*). Peace. Imperfect peace.

JORDAN. What news from the capitol?

MARCUS. God is dead and we are our own worst enemies.

JORDAN. I knew that.

MARCUS. Also there's a long-haired star approaching planet Earth.

JORDAN. The comet. Anthony told me.

MARCUS. I'll turn your bed around next week and we can watch it together. A ball of fire over the fire escape.

JORDAN. Promise?

MARCUS. I promise. We'll have a comet party.

JORDAN. We can go home by a different route.

MARCUS. We can.

JORDAN (*pause*). What else?

MARCUS. They're putting a large loading on my car insurance.

JORDAN. And?

MARCUS. Dr. Betty O'Gara laughed it off and went on eating the ends of her hair.

JORDAN. You adore her.

MARCUS. I adore her. I want her to sit on my face.

JORDAN. Nothing to be lost by asking her. You have a lovely face.

MARCUS (*reading rapidly from a periodical*). 'Late thirties single lady smoker in Portlaoise-Mountrath area seeks non-macho gent of same age or slightly older (must have own car), widowed or single, for chat, warmth, companionship, walks, whatever. All replies will be answered in confidence.'

JORDAN. God bless her and save her.

MARCUS (*as before*). 'Thank you, St. Clare, for three favours received. The third one was particularly appreciated. Holy Saint Clare, mystical bride of Saint Francis and friend to all who pray in a sincere and simple way for help from heaven, may my/our intentions be granted to me/us through the intercession of your grace and goodness, Amen. Say thirty times. Publication promised.'

JORDAN. So what was the third favour?

MARCUS. A's in the Junior Certificate. Or maybe she was over the thrush before the wedding night.

JORDAN. God bless her and save her. It calls for a poem.

MARCUS (*rummaging*). Ahh ha! This I like.

> *Barry, it is four years since I last kissed you.*
> *Ever since then, I have always missed you.*
> *Your face, your voice, your presence in the room.*
> *You are in my heart and you are in heaven, not in the tomb.'*

JORDAN. That's lovely.

MARCUS. No, it's not lovely. It's bloody awful.

JORDAN. It's lovely.

MARCUS. All right, it's lovely. It's the Sermon on the Mount.

JORDAN. It is, actually. Or part of it. (*Silence for a space.*) Do you know what my favourite dream was when I was a child? Except it wasn't a dream, exactly. It was what I liked to think about before I fell asleep.

MARCUS. Tell me.

JORDAN. I liked to think about my funeral mass.

MARCUS. Proceed, my son.

JORDAN. I liked to think how everybody would be crying and ashamed of themselves when the priest told them I had the stigmata. That's why I was slow and stupid and always in trouble, and why the nuns would kneel down and cross themselves when they heard me singing 'Bridge Over Troubled Waters'. Then Sister Maighréad would come up the aisle and breastfeed me there and then in the open coffin while the whole church prayed for forgiveness and hummed Taizé tunes. But it would be no use. I was gone for my heavenly banquet.

MARCUS. Sister Maighréad was lovely.

JORDAN. Did you have Sister Maighréad?

MARCUS. I gave her Toblerone one time and she lost a filling.

JORDAN. Did she leave or what?

MARCUS. She's an aromatherapist down in Athlone.

JORDAN. Go way. (*Pause.*) She was my first fantasy. I suppose she was twenty something. God be good to her.

MARCUS. Do you want to know what my first fantasy was?

JORDAN. I don't think so.

MARCUS. I used to lie awake and imagine that you and I were fighting back to back against Germans, mostly; sometimes the ancient Greeks. It depended what I was reading. And we ended up being killed together, and dying in each other's arms. It was wonderful. (*Pause.*) Were we normal?

JORDAN. Quite normal. Children are wise. They think about death all the time.

MARCUS. I suppose.

JORDAN. Dying together. The back to back thing.

MARCUS. Like the Spartans at Thermopylae.

JORDAN. You wouldn't do that, would you?

MARCUS. Do what?

JORDAN. You know what. Would you?

MARCUS. Yes . . . and no. No.

JORDAN. Good man.

MARCUS. Do you remember there was a time you were teaching me how to drive?

JORDAN. I do.

MARCUS. We were stopped in traffic at the bridge beside the obelisk.

JORDAN. Go on.

MARCUS. There was a Black Maria beside us.

JORDAN (*sings*). 'I shot the sheriff'.

MARCUS. You were about twenty. I was about eighteen. You can only be that happy when you're eighteen or twenty.

JORDAN *(sings)*. 'But I didn't shoot the deputy.'

MARCUS. Beer. Cigarettes. Women's skin and hair. Waking each morning with an erection. Your mother yanking the sheets off you to get you up.

JORDAN. I can't remember the verses.

MARCUS. We pulled in close to the Black Maria. We rolled down the windows. Then we turned the radio up to the point where we couldn't hear ourselves speak.

JORDAN. Bob Marley.

MARCUS. For the stupid fucker inside the van. The policeman driving it gave us a great grin.

JORDAN. All the drivers were smiling. God forgive us.

MARCUS. The morning they brought me back to the hospital after the overdose, I sat in the ambulance in a dressing gown somebody loaned me. My toenails were long and yellow. I hadn't cut them for a year. They were so far from my brain that I'd forgotten about them. And I was thinking would a nurse cut them for me because they wouldn't give a scissors to a man with my wrist. Then, after a while, the ambulance stopped and the traffic quietened around us. I could hear the cars in neutral and motorbikes passing and starlings too, but it was mostly silent. And suddenly, out there, out of nowhere, out of the world beyond me, I heard a Bob Marley song on a car radio. It was 'No Woman, No Cry.'

JORDAN. Great for the slow sets. Or on headphones with some excellent hash.

MARCUS. I looked down at the wires that bristled along the inside of my arm and I couldn't understand why the dressings were getting wet until I realised that the eyes in my face were streaming. Then I leaned my head into my lap and I prayed for forgiveness from that poor person in the back of the Black Maria.

JORDAN. He forgives you

MARCUS. How can you know that?

JORDAN. I know about ambulances.

MARCUS (*tenderly*). I know you do.

JORDAN. My worst moment was not in an ambulance. It was at the fancy dress in the club after the regatta when I was bringing drinks on a tray across the dining room. And the drummer in the band began this expectant drum-roll because I was staggering and there was fluid running from my mouth where all the sensation had gone. He thought I was drunk and he could tease me as I made it back to the table. When I did fall because I was weak in my legs, everybody cheered. And I knew then I was not going to be a doctor and that the next time these people assembled in such numbers would be for me. (*Pause.*) Do my drops.

MARCUS (*begins as before to drop ointment carefully into JORDAN's dehydrated sockets*). Here we go. Stare at the ceiling. Eyes wide open.

JORDAN. I do everything with my eyes wide open.

MARCUS. Are you up to this voodoo and vestments?

JORDAN. I am.

MARCUS. You don't believe it.

JORDAN. I want to believe it. I want to believe some of it. (*Pause.*) Am I smelling?

MARCUS. You stink. It's the odour of sanctity. (*Pause.*) What about the tape recording?

JORDAN. I'll do it. Don't let me smell.

MARCUS. When will you do it?

JORDAN. Soon. Spray something on me.

MARCUS. Soon is too late.

JORDAN. Tomorrow.

MARCUS. Tomorrow morning. Before your voice tires.

JORDAN. All right. In the morning. (*Pause.*) What'll I say?

MARCUS. Something ordinary. Deep things are no good when you're down. All we need is two minutes on a cassette.

JORDAN. And morphine.

MARCUS. And morphine.

JORDAN. A tape. For Mum. It's a good idea. You think?

MARCUS. Trust the electrical storm inside my head. Ever since the ECT, I think like lightning.

ARTHUR (*from the fire escape*). Permission to climb aboard?

MARCUS. Captain Haddock.

JORDAN. I'm not stale?

MARCUS. You're the word made fresh. (*Kisses him on the mouth.*) Now be good.

JORDAN. My breath?

MARCUS. The breath of life. Stop it.

ARTHUR (*appearing at the window*). I'm the first.

MARCUS. The one and only.

ARTHUR. The others are coming up the stairs as I speak. I just wanted to see which was quicker. (*To* JORDAN.) How's my *nearly* beloved?

JORDAN. Taking things lying down.

The door opens and the MOTHER *enters with* FATHER ANTHONY *and* MARCUS's *girlfriend* FELICITY. *One or other may be carrying a period chair for the mass.*

FATHER ANTHONY. Greetings from the Holy Ghost.

FELICITY. Hi.

MOTHER. Now. Felicity, this is my son Jordan. Chick, this is Felicity who is doing what she can for Marcus.

FELICITY (*to* MOTHER). Sorry?

JORDAN (*raises his arm to salute* FELICITY). Excuse me. Felicity –

FELICITY. Spellman. Not Jewish, actually. Not that I'd mind. But in case you wondered, at a mass and all.

MARCUS. No. He means excuse him. Being in bed.

FELICITY. Oh. No.

MOTHER. You know Father Anthony. But you haven't met Arthur. Arthur McLoughlin, our neighbour. Arthur thinks of himself as a member of the family. Don't you, Arthur?

ARTHUR. It's my privilege. Felicity means Happiness.

MARCUS (*delighted*). He went home to double-check it.

ARTHUR (*to* FELICITY). And you look it. You look the picture of happiness.

FELICITY. Thanks very much. I wish I was. My mum used to say she should have called me Dolores.

MARCUS. Miseries, Arthur. As in the dole.

ARTHUR (*to* FELICITY). Your mother was a Latinist?

FATHER ANTHONY. Her mother was a priest's daughter. Felicity's grandfather was a rector of the Church of Ireland in the Queen's County, County Laois. Her great grandmother was painted by John Butler Yeats.

FELICITY. We think, Mrs. McHenry.

MOTHER. Well, you've certainly got to know each other rather well in the space of ten minutes in a Fiat Cinquecento. Was the traffic very heavy?

FATHER ANTHONY. In fact, we were chatting mostly about the psychic Felicity goes to.

MOTHER. Psychic? You attend a psychic?

MARCUS. Better than psychiatrist. Shrink from psychiatry.

MOTHER (*spraying the aerosol freshener*). Does she have a crystal ball?

FELICITY. No. She has a lap-top. I mean, she does look into the future . . .

JORDAN. All that lies ahead of us are the lies we told each other in the past.

FELICITY. That's the sort of thing she'd say. It's harmless, really. Fortune cookie stuff.

MARCUS. Now you've gone and hurt Jordan's feelings. He was being profound.

FELICITY. Oh, Lord. (*She sits down in a natural way on the bed.*) This is Felicity all over. I was only trying to defend astrologers a bit, because everyone thinks they're complete phoneys, but mine was right about three big things in my life and about the Pope's Parkinson's too before anybody else was.

FATHER ANTHONY. We're only teasing you.

ARTHUR. Very affectionately too. You remind me of a girl my son Rodney went out with. But then the fool drifted off to Canada. Don't talk to me about it.

MARCUS. We don't.

MOTHER. Marcus!

FELICITY (*to* JORDAN). Am I sitting on your leg?

JORDAN. No. You're fine.

FELICITY. I'm sitting on something. Maybe it's only a jar.

JORDAN. It's what I piss in.

FELICITY. I'm so sorry.

MARCUS. No problem.

FELICITY. I didn't spill anything? . . . I mean. God, what do I mean?

JORDAN. You mean well. (*She makes to get up.*) Sit. Stay. (*She does.*)

FATHER ANTHONY. I think we'll make a start. (*At the night table.*) This will do perfectly for our purposes. So. (*He adjusts it. The* MOTHER *lays a white embroidered cloth on it.*) That's really beautiful. It's an heirloom.

MOTHER (*pleased*). Far from it, indeed.

ARTHUR. You wouldn't see it in (*Phonating.*) Aras an Uachtaráin.

MARCUS. Spoken like a native.

ARTHUR. I am a native.

FATHER ANTHONY. We have our candle. No crystal ball, unfortunately.

FELICITY. Don't.

FATHER ANTHONY. We have bread and we have wine.

MARCUS. We have a gong. A big bongy gong. (*He sits into the wheelchair.*)

FATHER ANTHONY. Pass on the gong. We have the bread and wine of the scriptures, Torah and Testament. (*Places a Bible down.*) I should say that I asked Jordan what bread he would like to break this afternoon, and he said brown bread. The brown bread his mother always made. But she has emphatically refused to bake for this occasion, so we're stuck with these silly wafers.

MOTHER. It wouldn't be natural. Show me any bishop in the country who'd have brown bread on his altar. Besides, we should be setting an example to . . . Arthur and Felicity.

FATHER ANTHONY (*places a casette tape recorder beside him*). Terrific. Wagons in a circle, like so. (*Kisses a stole, slips it round his neck and sits nearest* JORDAN. *The others seat themselves too.*)

FELICITY. Just a tick. (*She uses an inhaler.*) Sorry. I get caught up when I feel uncomfortable. What I mean is-

FATHER ANTHONY. You're fine. Tutto va bene. Now.

He starts the recorder. We hear the delicate soundtrack from Picnic at Hanging Rock *as an accompaniment.*

The Lord be with you.

OMNES. And also with you.

FATHER ANTHONY. We meet as a little community to
   do two things that are fundamental to human beings
   everywhere. We meet to tell stories and to share food. The
   stories are about Jesus the Jew. We call them the Gospels.
   There are also the stories of the Hebrew Bible which Jesus
   himself heard as a boy and which shaped his life, his death,
   and his . . .

MOTHER. Resurrection.

FATHER ANTHONY. His risenness. All these stories, old and
   new, feed and nourish us. The meal we share is a feast of
   bread and wine. When we eat and drink this bread and
   wine, as Jesus asked us to do when we come together to
   remember him, we receive Christ into our lives. God feeds
   us with his own flesh and blood in the very same way that a
   mother feeds her unborn baby with the flesh and bloodstream
   of her body. And we ourselves become the body of Christ,
   the flesh and blood of the mystery of God in the world.

   So we are more than we imagine. We are the children of the
   spirit of the God of Jesus of Nazareth. We may not have
   time for God. God has eternity as a playground for us.
   We may not believe in God. God believes in us. We may
   not love God. God adores us. And, insofar as we love one
   another, especially those we cannot bring ourselves to like,
   then we are loving God face to face.

   Along with our stories and our food, we offer our fears, our
   fragilities, our mistakes, our regrets, our rationalisations of
   those regrets. We say: Lord, have mercy.

MOTHER/JORDAN. Lord, have mercy.

FATHER ANTHONY. Christ, have mercy.

MOTHER/JORDAN/ARTHUR/FELICITY. Christ, have mercy.

FATHER ANTHONY. Lord, have mercy.

MOTHER/JORDAN/ARTHUR/FELICITY. Lord, have mercy.

FATHER ANTHONY. Felicity is going to break the scripture.

FELICITY. O, Lord.

FATHER ANTHONY. A very good beginning. (*Passes her the Bible and places his stole around her neck.*)

FELICITY (*scanning*). 'This is the word of the Lord, the word of your creator, O Jacob, of him who fashioned you, Israel.' Is that right?

FATHER ANTHONY. Perfect.

MARCUS. Is that all?

JORDAN. Shh.

FELICITY (*fluent; intent*). 'I have called you by name and you are my own. When you pass through deep waters, I am with you, when you pass through torrents, they will not sweep you away. For I am the Lord your God, the Holy One of Israel, your deliverer. Cease to dwell on days gone by, and to brood over ancient history. Here and now I will do a new thing. This moment it will break from the bud. Can you not perceive it?'

FATHER ANTHONY *accepts the Bible and stole from* FELICITY *and passes them to the* MOTHER. *The* MOTHER *bundles the stole in her lap as she scans the page.*

MOTHER. The response to the psalm is: I cried aloud to God.

OMNES. I cried aloud to God.

MOTHER.
In the day of my distress I sought the Lord,
And by night I lifted my outspread hands in prayer.
I lay sweating and nothing would cool me;
I refused all comfort.
I cried aloud to God.

FATHER ANTHONY. I cried aloud to God.

MOTHER.
When I called God to mind, I groaned;
As I lay thinking, darkness came over my spirit.
My eyelids were tightly closed;
I was dazed. I couldn't speak. (*She is breaking down.*)

MARCUS. I cried aloud to God. (MARCUS *takes the Bible from her and reads*.)

My thoughts went back to times long past,
I remembered forgotten years;
All night long I was in deep distress,
As I lay thinking, my spirit was sunk in despair.

JORDAN.
I cried aloud to God.

Silence. The MOTHER *composes herself. The music plays. A breeze from the garden lifts the curtain.*

FATHER ANTHONY (*puts the stole around his neck and places the Bible beside him. He has the Gospel story by heart*). Our Gospel comes from Mark, the earliest, the oldest, the saddest, the shortest, and in ways the strangest of the four Gospels. It's a story some people haven't liked, because it seems to imply that Jesus wasn't always successful in curing the sick straight away.

'The people brought a blind man to Jesus and begged him to touch him. He took the blind man by the hand and led him away out of the village. Then he spat on his eyes, laid his hands upon him, and asked whether he could see anything. The man's sight began to come back, and he said, "I see men; they look like trees, but they are walking about." Jesus laid his hands on his eyes again; he looked hard, and now he was cured so that he saw everything clearly.'

MOTHER. Praise to thee, Lord Jesus Christ.

JORDAN *has begun slowly to massage his temple with his fingers; but nobody notices.*

FATHER ANTHONY. Lord, sometimes we find it difficult to believe that you have called us, each and every one of us, by our first name. We find it hard to understand that you long for us and belong with us. Sometimes we can't sleep, can't pray. We lie awake in the darkness.

Lord, hear us then.

ARTHUR. Lord, in your mercy hear our prayer.

FATHER ANTHONY. Lord, we can't see very far at times. We can make out figures walking like trees, the tree of life, the wood of the cross, but no more. We need new vision, second sight. Lord, hear us.

MOTHER/MARCUS/ FELICITY. Lord, graciously hear us.

JORDAN*'s face has creased into lines of pain. Nobody sees.*

FATHER ANTHONY. Would anyone like to pray?

ARTHUR. I would like to pray that, this time next year or D.V. as my secretary used to say, Jordan will be in the thick of the Dragon fleet awaiting the starting gun.

MOTHER. Lord, hear us.

OMNES. Lord, graciously hear us.

ARTHUR. Amen.

FELICITY. I would like to pray about the comet. Not in terms of astrology, obviously! But that we would look up from our hands at times to see the whole host of heaven watching us, and perhaps find a star there that would lead us to where God is hiding in our lives. (*Pause. They're all looking at her.*) Lord, in your mercy

OMNES. Lord, graciously hear us/Lord, in your mercy, hear our prayer.

FATHER ANTHONY. I'd like to pray for Jordan's mother.

MARCUS. She's my mother too.

FATHER ANTHONY. She is indeed – and she's off to Lough Derg at the weekend to make a retreat and be alone for a time.

MOTHER. When am I not alone?

MARCUS. Lough Derg? As in self-inflicted whippings?

MOTHER. You wouldn't recognise Lough Derg if it spat in your face.

ARTHUR. Beautiful place for sailing, though. Wouldn't mind it myself.

FATHER ANTHONY. No. That's another Lough Derg. But perhaps we ought to gather ourselves and go on. Let us pray.

JORDAN *sits bolt upright and howls, holding the cry as long as possible. The tumour has invaded a nerve. Everyone turns to stare at him. Blackout.*

ACT TWO

Scene One

Setting as before. A week has passed. The windows are wide open on a warm summer's midnight.

The room is in darkness apart from the lighthouse glow of the set which illuminates JORDAN *asleep. Perhaps we can hear the American* Health and Fitness *TV programme he's been watching, alongside the rock and roll music from downstairs with bursts of party laughter and shouting that continue throughout the scene.*

FELICITY*'s head appears outside the window at the fire escape. She taps on the windowpane, but* JORDAN *can't hear. Then she calls out.*

FELICITY. Jordan! Jordan!

JORDAN. Where?

FELICITY. It's me. Felicity. Can I come in?

JORDAN. Always.

FELICITY (*enters in party mode. She's drunk but it only softens her.*). I'm knackered. I swear to God. The heat. (*Hiccups.*) Where's the absent host?

JORDAN. The dark horse Marcus.

FELICITY. I swear to you. He invited around a dozen people. Max. The others must have overheard.

JORDAN. The Last Supper has turned into the feeding of the multitude. Good theology.

FELICITY. You should hear (*Hiccups.*) some of the accents.

JORDAN. Jesus would have said 'I done'.

FELICITY. If you saw them.

JORDAN. Let me see you. (*He uses the remote control to turn down the TV.*)

FELICITY. I'm not, you know, bollocksed or blotto. I'm just . . . what other word for drunk begins with a B?

JORDAN. Sit.

FELICITY (*she sits beside him*). But . . . but with a B. How about: I have the best brand for both of us buddies. (*She takes out a rolled joint.*)

JORDAN. Ahh ha!

FELICITY. Ahh ha is right, my friend. Wait a mo. (*She uses her inhaler deeply.*) Clear the old lungs first. (*Lights the joint.*) Now, my brother.

JORDAN. In law?

FELICITY. Be good. (*She inhales and holds the joint to JORDAN's lips.*) This is top of the range. Lebanese. No less. No asparagus in this lot.

JORDAN. Umm.

FELICITY. Umm is right. (*She takes another draw and sits peacably watching the TV.*) Does anyone actually buy those health and fitness gadgets? And the jargon – abs and pecs. Desist. (*Pause.*) But I'd love her figure, so I would.

JORDAN. Yours is perfect.

FELICITY (*to the set*). Those boobs are not natural. You could draw a map of the world on both of them. (*Laughs as one does on dope.*) Are you a tit man or a bum man, Jordan?

JORDAN. With me it was never a question of either/or. It was more a matter of both/and.

FELICITY. Say no more.

JORDAN. Felicity. Can I ask you something? Something the same but . . . different.

FELICITY. Ask away.

JORDAN. Do you believe in the Real Presence?

FELICITY. Yep. Course I do. (*She exhales blissfully.*)

JORDAN. Are you sure?

FELICITY. Sure I'm sure.

JORDAN. You're not really supposed to, you know. As a Protestant.

FELICITY (*she inhales again, holds it, exhales*). Listen. When you think about it, where in the world is Jesus Christ *not* really present? (*Pause; to the television.*) Do men actually like women with boobs that big?

JORDAN. I don't know.

FELICITY. Well, you should. You're a man; and a fine specimen too, may I say.

JORDAN. No, I meant about the Real Presence. I don't know. And I want to.

FELICITY (*offering* JORDAN *the joint*). More?

JORDAN. Please.

FELICITY (*happily*). Why do they call it dope when it makes you so intelligent?

She holds the joint for him as he draws. Music continues from downstairs: the party is in full session. A pause.

Tell me about before.

JORDAN. Before I became a morphine addict, I was a medical student.

FELICITY. Like father, like son. Did you love him?

JORDAN. My dad? No. Not at the time. I do now.

FELICITY. That's terrible.

JORDAN. He knew it. That I didn't.

FELICITY. That's worse, even.

JORDAN. Does he know it now? That I do?

FELICITY. I don't know, Jordan. (*Inhales.*) But I think that if God loves us as much as he says he does, then he won't let any of us get lost in the darkness.

JORDAN. But he let himself get lost.

FELICITY. So he's a good guide. (*Pause.*) Marcus told me about looking in through a porthole at your dad operating.

JORDAN. It's true. I was with him.

FELICITY. When I was little, I used to sit at my Daddy's feet and comb his legs, they were so hairy. And he'd write my name each day on a banana because he loved the feel of the nib of the pen as it sank in the soft skin. Then nobody at school could steal them at lunchtime. (*Laughs; reflects. A pause.*) Are you afraid, ever? Sometimes I'm afraid all the time.

JORDAN. It's a mistake to take your life too personally.

FELICITY. How should we live our lives then, wise one?

JORDAN. Without comparing and contrasting them; and by being contented with our own unhappiness.

FELICITY. That's not enough. That's not enough to live for or to die for. I need more than that.

JORDAN (*great anguish; cries out*). I do too.

FELICITY (*reaches to him*). I know you do, pet. You poor, poor Jordan. I know. (*Pause.* FELICITY *feels her head.*) Now I feel sick.

JORDAN. You're in the right place. I'm almost a doctor. I answered a question on tumours of the brain on a multiple-choice paper in my third year. Now I have one. A subarachnoid astracytoma.

FELICITY. I feel sweaty and shitty and sick. I think I'm going to throw up.

JORDAN. In under the bed. A pot.

FELICITY. Fuck it. I *am* going to throw up. (*She puts the joint aside, unbuttons her top and takes it off in case she stains it.*

Then she gets down on her hands and knees and feels under the bed with her arm. True enough, there's a pot within reach.) Oh God. Oh Jesus. (*To* JORDAN.) Hold my hair back, Jordan.

JORDAN. I can't. (*She throws her hair over her head onto the bed and bows to the pot.*) Good girl.

FELICITY. So sorry. So, so sorry. Sweat. (*And she vomits into the pot abundantly, then kneels beside the bed with her head on the duvet while* JORDAN *strokes her hair with his hand.*) Bold, bad Felicity.

JORDAN. Better soon.

FELICITY. Wicked, wicked woman.

JORDAN. Don't be sad.

FELICITY. I'll never smoke dope again.

JORDAN. Me neither.

FELICITY. Lebanese, my arse. (*Laughs.*)

JORDAN. I thought you looked foreign. (*Pause.*) Maybe the wine was off.

FELICITY. The red was lovely. And the white. It must have been the G and T's. The lemon looked strange.

JORDAN. Morphine is nicer than booze. Or marijuana.

FELICITY. Where is it? (*Gets up, rummages at the night-table, finds it, and walks to the window with the joint in one hand, the pot in the other.*) May I?

JORDAN. Hmm?

FELICITY. You know. I'm mortified. Even my breasts have gone red.

JORDAN. Fire ahead. The poor rhododendrons.

FELICITY (*she empties the pot out the window*). My body is cold and trembly. But my face is hot. I'm wet all over. (*Pause.*) Thanks be to God your mother is in Lough Derg.

JORDAN. Cold and trembly and wet all over.

FELICITY. What will she find there?

JORDAN. This room.

FELICITY. What will she bring back?

JORDAN. Corn plasters. A chest infection. Faith, hope, charity. These three.

FELICITY. You love your mother. Marcus hates her.

JORDAN. I was the first. He was the second. He thinks he's a semi-finalist.

FELICITY. No. It's not that . . . complicated.

JORDAN. They will make their peace over my dead body.

FELICITY (*Laughs*). God forgive you. (*Pause.*) You can be cruel. Marcus can be cruel too.

JORDAN. To you?

FELICITY. No. Unless you count wearing a thong.

JORDAN. A thong?

FELICITY. He makes me wear thongs. He's bought me four already. Mauve, lemon, white and black. They cut into you a bit, but he won't stand for Sloggies. I can't believe I do what he tells me. It must be my hormones. All the eggs inside me, waiting to be great-grandfathers and great-grandmothers in a hundred years' time. (*Pause.*) Sometimes he's so sad, Marcus. As if he'd just made love to me. But he hasn't.

JORDAN. I know.

FELICITY. I can't look at his wrists, Jordan. Is that wrong of me?

JORDAN. No. If you didn't love him, you'd be dying to see.

FELICITY. And I thought that, if we were to make love, if we were to be entirely naked – not just nude, you know, but naked – I would make him wear a woman's long white gloves all the way up his arms to his shoulders, so that . . . but then, of course, my own fingertips would still be able to feel them through the thinness of the material.

JORDAN. He wants you to kiss them, doesn't he? As a test.

FELICITY. You think? (*Pause.*) Anyway. And now, for my next trick . . .

Easily, effortlessly, she slips into a series of tai chi exercises that are slow, spellbound, balletic. The music from downstairs ought to match this shift of mood so that something like an epiphany, an event of rapture, occurs before our eyes. When it ends, there is silence. JORDAN raises his arm in applause.

Marcus has never seen me do that. (*She comes to the bedside and kneels.*) Are you very warm?

JORDAN. Umm.

FELICITY. You're wet through.

JORDAN. Am.

FELICITY. Wait till we see. (*She takes the hairdryer from the hostess trolley and finds a socket.*) Now. (*She kneels beside JORDAN and turns the hairdryer on. At first she directs the flow of cool air onto his forehead and face. Then she peels the covers back as far as his waist, opens the buttons of his pyjama top and cools his chest. Finally she removes the duvet altogether to reveal the adult diaper that JORDAN wears. He doesn't attempt to stop her. She uses the hairdryer around the nappy, inside it, and down the length of his legs to the tips of his toes.*)

Well?

JORDAN. Very.

FELICITY. The Lord be with you.

JORDAN. And also with you.

FELICITY. Shall I change you?

JORDAN. I'm changed.

FELICITY. Are you sure?

JORDAN. Umm.

FELICITY (*sniffs herself*). Then it must be me.

JORDAN. No. I could have twenty bed baths in a day and I'd still smell of shit.

FELICITY. Listen. My feet are so bad I bring a change of shoes and a spray-can with me. We're human beings being human. (*Silence. They listen to the music, the night sounds.*) I wish I could carry you in my arms to the window. But you're too big and strong.

JORDAN. To see the comet?

FELICITY. No. Fuck the comet. That's only fireworks. To see the night.

JORDAN. Beautiful.

FELICITY. Yes. The night is beautiful. The darkness is beautiful.

JORDAN. When I was able to close my eyes, the veins in my eyelids were like rivers. I could have given them names.

FELICITY. Down in the darkness of the garden, the trees are breathing out; and here in the darkness of the bedroom, you and I are breathing in. Aren't they clever, though, to be making oxygen out of our poor carbon dioxide. Aren't they fierce clever all together?

JORDAN. They are.

FELICITY. That's what God does best. God breathes in our carbon dioxide and breathes out pure air.

JORDAN (*after a pause*). I had three friends, Felicity.

FELICITY. As many as that.

JORDAN. Mile. Pacha. Bero.

FELICITY. Tell me.

JORDAN. Mile was a man. A Croatian; a Catholic. Pacha was a Bosnian woman. A Muslim. And Bero, he was an

Orthodox Serb. The four of us backpacked together. In
Greece. Ten years ago. Ten years ago this summer solstice.
One day in the Peloponnese . . .

He grimaces in pain

FELICITY. Take your time.

JORDAN. We hired a pedalo. Let it drift by itself half a mile
out. Until we couldn't hear the beach. I looked over the
side. I could see a hundred metres down. Bright as a
greenhouse to the bottom.

FELICITY. Go on.

JORDAN. We had bread and wine. And cigarettes. We all
stripped off. We floated for hours. Farther and farther out.
Pacha swam in a white cotton frock because of her sunburn.

FELICITY. And?

JORDAN. Nothing.

FELICITY. Nothing? You didn't cast lots and eat the unlucky
one?

JORDAN. No.

FELICITY. What, then?

JORDAN. Later.

FELICITY. Later.

JORDAN. Couldn't sleep. Mosquito bites. My blood on the
ceiling of the room. Climbed to the roof of the pension.
(*Pause.*) Pacha.

FELICITY. The Bosnian woman.

JORDAN. We took bedsheets off the washing line. Dry, clean
sheets in the cool night air. We lay down there. Under the
wooden pegs and the starlight. With the horns of motorcars
honking in the deep streets beneath us.

FELICITY. Was she nice to you?

JORDAN. Very.

FELICITY. Was it beautiful?

JORDAN. Utterly.

FELICITY. Just perfect.

JORDAN. Imperfect. But pure. Pure and imperfect.

FELICITY. Did you cry?

JORDAN. Yes.

FELICITY. You're crying now.

JORDAN. I can't be.

FELICITY. You are. Your grey-green eyes are filling with tears. I can see far down into them. A hundred metres down.

JORDAN. Not the eye-drops?

FELICITY. Not the eye-drops. You. Not your body. You. The river of Jordan.

JORDAN. Eucharisto.

FELICITY. Hmm?

JORDAN. Eucharisto. The Greek. The Greek for Thank You.

He will not speak again. There is a tender, truthful pause. Then ARTHUR *appears out of nowhere on the fire-escape.*

ARTHUR. Felicity!

FELICITY (*shocked*). Jesus Christ.

ARTHUR. Sorry.

FELICITY (*winded, sits on the floor clutching herself*). You nearly killed me. My heart stopped for a moment. You eejit.

ARTHUR. I said sorry. I wouldn't be surprised if I dropped dead myself. I'm that . . . traumatised. Can I come in? (*He does so.*) I couldn't get through the front door. It's locked with the chain on. One of the windows in the drawing room is broken. There must be three hundred people cavorting in the house. In the garden. My next door neighbour's called the police.

FELICITY (*throws her top on and buttons it*). For Christ's sake, where's Marcus?

ARTHUR. Then I thought: if the police arrive to clear the premises, they might see my greenhouse. They might see the cannabis. What in God's name am I going to do if they see the cannabis?

FELICITY. Say it's your son's.

ARTHUR. I can't. How is he going to get custody of my grandchildren if he's wanted over here on a narcotics charge? They'll end up with that Serbian warlord.

FELICITY. Arthur, they are not going to arrest a respectable Methodist with one of the best addresses in Dublin.

Pummelling on the bedroom door. ARTHUR *throws himself against it.*

ARTHUR. Get out of here! You're not getting in. There's a very sick man in here.

VOICE OF MARCUS. There's a very sick man out here as well. Let go.

FELICITY. It's Marcus. Let him in.

ARTHUR. Marcus. Is that you?

MARCUS *beats a Beethoven's Fifth on the door.* ARTHUR *opens it.* MARCUS *enters dressed as a beduoin in flowing white garments. He is elated.*

MARCUS. It is I. Laurence of Suburbia!

FELICITY (*shriek of laughter*). Marcus!

ARTHUR. Good God!

MARCUS. Ireland is a cultural desert. I dress accordingly.

ARTHUR. I think you're mad. I think you're both mad. I can understand it in you, Marcus, but I'm flabbergasted by you, Felicity. We're in the middle of a riot.

FELICITY (*to* MARCUS). Arthur's terrified the fuzz are going to find his cannabis crop.

MARCUS. Tell them it's mine, Captain Haddock. I'll get away with diminished responsibility because I killed my father and slept with my mother. Besides, it's time I gave a little bit back to the community. After all, the community has done so much for me.

ARTHUR. Your home is invaded. Your property is vandalised. A dying man is disturbed.

MARCUS. Nothing disturbs a dying man.

ARTHUR. Think of your mother. How would your mother feel?

MARCUS. Not as badly as she's bound to feel on Lough Derg. (*Pause.*) Now. Logistics. I made a promise. (*He stands at the foot of* JORDAN*'s bed, assessing it.*) I may be wrong about this. It could have been a 747 in flames on the way to Shannon. But it looked very like a comet crossing the Hibernian desert. In which case.

FELICITY. The comet! Where?

ARTHUR (*at the window*). There are people in my side-passage! On my patio!

MARCUS. A star from the east is lighting our way to the stable. And if it stops over this city and stands still there, I will become a Christian.

FELICITY. You are a Christian.

MARCUS. No, I'm not. I am not a part of Christ incarnate. I am only a piece of Christianity Incorporated.

ARTHUR. Christ Almighty, the police are in my garden! What am I going to do?

MARCUS. Tonight, you see, in a place of utter bedlam within walking distance of this room, a fifteen-year old addict is squeezing her baby into the world. (*He tugs hard at the bedstead.*)

FELICITY. Leave it, Marcus. Don't. He couldn't give a shit about the comet. Marcus, he'll fall out.

MARCUS. Nobody falls tonight. Everybody rises.

ARTHUR. Think, Arthur, think!

MARCUS. Feel, Arthur, feel! Old men who watch parked cars by night, like shepherds watching their flocks, they are standing around the infant in an honour guard.

FELICITY. Marcus! Stop it! You haven't insight. Not tonight.

MARCUS. And the afterbirth steams like incense on the tarmacadam.

ARTHUR. I'll have to go, Felicity. I'll go and then I'll come back. Not to be continued!

He clambers out. MARCUS *lifts the bottom of the bed off the ground.*

FELICITY. Be careful!

MARCUS. If we can't see the comet, we can at least watch Arthur being pistol-whipped by the Gardaí Síochána. (*He pulls the bed away from the wall.*)

FELICITY. Easy! Easy!

MARCUS. Nothing's easy. (*And he turns the bed in one slow but fluent movement towards the window.* JORDAN*'s cover slips from him; he is a diapered ragdoll.*) So!

FELICITY (*stooping to pick up the sheets before coming to the window too*). Where? Where is it? What do you see?

MARCUS. Jordan! Jordan, look! There. Five to twelve. Five to twelve. Can you see?

JORDAN *emits a cry.*

FELICITY. I see it too, I think. I think I do.

MARCUS. We have lived to see it. Now lettest thou thy servants depart in peace, O Lord.

The three of them go on staring up at the sky. The light fades slowly.

Scene Two

*Two weeks later. The windows are closed, the curtains open to
let in moonlight. The* MOTHER *and* FATHER ANTHONY *are
sitting together on one side of the room; on the other, under a
single white sheet,* JORDAN *is sleeping deeply as if in a coma.
The conversation is very quiet. The* MOTHER *is embroidering
a cover for a piano stool.*

FATHER ANTHONY. I've never been there. I should go. I've
never been up Croagh Patrick either. Or to Knock. There are
so many things in my life I haven't got round to. Yet.

MOTHER. Lough Derg is not really meant for people like us.

FATHER ANTHONY. Ah.

MOTHER. You can't say that, of course.

FATHER ANTHONY. I suppose not.

MOTHER. Very good people go.

FATHER ANTHONY. The best. Salt of the earth.

MOTHER. But very . . . Fianna Fáil.

FATHER ANTHONY. Sure. (*Pause.*) The Duke of Norfolk
goes to Lough Derg.

MOTHER. I suppose he has to.

FATHER ANTHONY. There's that.

MOTHER. Mostly women there.

FATHER ANTHONY. Women at the Annunciation. Women at
the tomb.

MOTHER (*Pause*). Do you miss Rwanda?

FATHER ANTHONY. No.

MOTHER. I'd never heard of it. Rwanda. You must have seen
terrible things.

FATHER ANTHONY. I must have.

MOTHER (*pause*). Embroidery is a great companion.

FATHER ANTHONY. My mother knits.

MOTHER. Knits?

FATHER ANTHONY. Yeah.

MOTHER. She's alive then?

FATHER ANTHONY. Yes.

MOTHER. Why is it, do you think, that so many men leave the priesthood when their mother dies?

FATHER ANTHONY. Do they?

MOTHER. Umm. For one reason or another.

FATHER ANTHONY. Ahh.

MOTHER. Punch or Judy.

FATHER ANTHONY. Punch or Judy?

MOTHER. Old seminary slang. Before your time. Alcohol or women. Or men. This is almost the millennium.

FATHER ANTHONY (*Pause*). Rwanda. You were saying.

MOTHER. Was I? (*She leaves the thread in her lap and rubs her eyes.*)

FATHER ANTHONY (*pause*). Atrocities you can . . . process. It's the dreariness of daily life that defeats you.

MOTHER (*still rubbing*). I don't understand you.

FATHER ANTHONY. I don't always understand myself. When I came home, or when I came back, they offered me counselling. I suppose I do lie awake at night, thinking; but it's not about machetes. It's about my own resentments, my own desires.

MOTHER. Desires?

FATHER ANTHONY. No, no, no. Living without women is easy. It's living with men that's so hard.

MOTHER. That I can understand.

FATHER ANTHONY. Trying to teach thirteen-year-old boys gives you grey hairs. Not massacres upriver. They make you feel . . . alive.

MOTHER. Does Jordan make you feel alive?

FATHER ANTHONY. In a different way. Jordan has done more for me than I could ever do for him. Because of his faith.

MOTHER (*stops embroidering; looks at the priest*). Don't you have faith?

FATHER ANTHONY. I have many beliefs. It's not always the same thing. Jordan dwells in the mystery of God; I seem to live in the mystifications of theology.

MOTHER (*sharply*). Have you said anything to him that might mar his faith?

FATHER ANTHONY. Of course not.

MOTHER (*pause; appeased*). It's your age talking. How old are you, Anthony?

FATHER ANTHONY. Forty-five.

MOTHER. The Roaring Forties.

FATHER ANTHONY. Perhaps it's because we're not meant to live this long. Human bodies have been dying at forty years of age for the past hundred thousand years. Suddenly we have disinfectants, antibiotics, the VHI. We can hit eighty, no bother. But the soul is tired. The soul is worn out. The soul wants to bow down to the good ground and give in.

MOTHER. Jordan is thirty. Even younger than Jesus.

FATHER ANTHONY. Forgive me. I wasn't thinking.

MOTHER. When he dies, my grandchildren die with him.

FATHER ANTHONY. I'm so sorry.

MOTHER. I'm left with my philosopher; and all I can do about him is to be . . . philosophical.

JORDAN makes an inarticulate sound. His MOTHER *goes to him, checks him, returns.*

FATHER ANTHONY. I should go.

MOTHER. Yes. The next stage, when it comes, will be the last.

FATHER ANTHONY. How can you tell?

MOTHER. I was a nurse. A Vincent's nurse. After the coma, the breathing. They call it Cheyne-Stoking.

FATHER ANTHONY. Cheyne . . . ?

MOTHER. I suppose Cheyne was a doctor and Stoke was a doctor. I don't know. My husband used to say: those who chain-smoke will Cheyne-Stoke. He was very proud of his witticisms.

FATHER ANTHONY. Then I should stay.

MOTHER. No. This is between the two of us, just like his birth. I'll see you down to the door.

FATHER ANTHONY. Would you like me to . . . pray? With you. For him.

MOTHER. No. I'm tired of prayers. And he's had the last sacrament so many times it means nothing any more.

FATHER ANTHONY. I'll see myself out, Martha. You look so tired. Your eyes look so tired.

MOTHER. They're dry. I cry when I'm watching *Casualty* on the TV; but I'm dry-eyed when my son is dying.

FATHER ANTHONY. Sit. Please. Stay. Rest. I'll go.

MOTHER. No. I like to walk around the house at night. It's my happiest memory of this home. I used to walk around it in the small hours, listening at the doors to hear the breathing of my two babies.

They leave the room, closing the door quietly behind them. We hear it being locked from outside. Stillness and silence. JORDAN*'s breathing is becoming louder, more laboured and, at the same time, much more intermittent. Whole* *periods pass without any inhalation. We hear the sound of the outer doorknob being turned without success, then some uncertain tapping.*

FELICITY (*from outside*). Mrs. McHenry. (*Pause.*) Mrs. McHenry. It's Felicity. Are you there?

MARCUS (*from outside*). Mum. It's me. Can you open up?

FELICITY (*from outside*). I wonder did she fall asleep? She must be exhausted.

MARCUS (*from outside*). Nothing exhausts my mother.

FELICITY. Could she be cleaning him?

MARCUS (*vexed*). Who's this 'him'? You mean Jordan.

FELICITY (*louder*). Mrs. McHenry!

MARCUS (*from outside*). Mum!

MOTHER (*from outside, angry*). Are you trying to wake the dead or what?

FELICITY (*from outside*). We thought you were asleep inside.

MOTHER (*from outside*). Can I not go to the toilet in my own home without a search party?

MARCUS (*from outside*). Why did you lock the door? Why?

The key turns in the lock and the door opens.

MOTHER (*in doorway*). To give him peace and quiet. That's why.

MARCUS (*in doorway*). I want to go in.

MOTHER. All I want is a few minutes.

MARCUS. All *I* want is a few minutes.

MOTHER. Your father died on a toilet bowl. When I found him, he was in rigor mortis. All I ask is a little while to be left alone with someone who's still alive.

FELICITY (*pause*). We'll wait below, Mrs. McHenry.

MARCUS (*pause*). I'll be downstairs. Call me.

He steps into the room, bows toward the bed, turns and goes out. The MOTHER *closes the door, stands against it, slides slowly to the floor and sits there with her head in her hands.* JORDAN *continues the characteristic respiration of a dying person during which the* MOTHER *moves on her hands and knees to the bedside.*

MOTHER. That's right, my prince, my sweetheart. Push. Push. Push with the pain. Push down. Push deeper. You wouldn't leave me. Push. For eighteen hours you wouldn't leave me. Push, my pet, my darling, my dearest. You loved being in me. You loved being there. Now push. My lips were bleeding. The good gas in my mouth. Pressing and pushing. You held on hard. (*She cries the long, low ululation of a woman in labour.*) Push now. Push. The blue world welcomes you, my honey one, my happiness. You wouldn't leave me. I cried out, Come!

JORDAN's *breathing has stopped and so does her strange childbirthing. She kneels before her son. The bedroom door opens softly and* MARCUS *steps in. The lights fade.*

EPILOGUE

Three days have passed. It is the late afternoon/early evening of JORDAN'*s funeral.* MOTHER *and* FELICITY *are alone together in the bedroom.* FELICITY *is studying the titles on the bookshelves while the barefoot* MOTHER *is stripping the sheets off the bed. She wears kitchen gloves over the black sleeves of her mourning clothes. The windows are wide open.*

FELICITY (*looking at a spine*). *The Canterbury Tales* by Geoffrey Chaucer. I always meant to read *The Canterbury Tales*.

MOTHER (*not turning*). Take it.

FELICITY. Lord, no. I was only saying . . . he was a great reader.

MOTHER. I suppose he was.

FELICITY. *The Documents of Vatican II* by . . . it doesn't say who.

MOTHER. Do you want it?

FELICITY. Gracious, no. He must have been really brainy.

MOTHER. I'm in two minds about reading. Marcus was a great reader. But he couldn't read the writing on the wall.

FELICITY (*pause*). Weren't the bidding prayers that he wrote just brilliant?

MOTHER. My mind was elsewhere.

FELICITY. He wrote that beautiful one about you. It was in the Order of Service. Everybody was talking about it afterwards and even in the graveyard.

MOTHER. I think, Felicity, it was probably Jordan's day.

FELICITY (*dismayed*). No, of course, what I meant was that . . .

A pause. FELICITY *uses her inhaler: two short bursts. The* MOTHER *opens a wardrobe from which she takes a bundle of* JORDAN's *clothes; stares at them for a time, then inhales them greedily, pressing them to her face. Then she's irresolute. She slips them into a black bag.* FELICITY *is still studying books. She has seen nothing.*

FELICITY. *The Jade Grotto, Volume II: Vintage Victorian Erotica.* Gosh.

MOTHER. Marcus.

FELICITY. Actually, it says Jordan.

MOTHER. That's Marcus's sense of humour.

FELICITY. He's heart-broken.

MOTHER. I know he is. But hearts have a way of mending. That's what makes us human. Elephants die of their grief, you know. Elephant keepers don't. The problem is not the human heart. It's the human mind. (*She lifts more of* JORDAN's *clothing to her face, stops, then drops them into the black bag.*)

FELICITY (*turns to the* MOTHER *too late to see it*). Marcus is sickeningly sane.

MOTHER. Can you not imagine how much it would mean to me to have a daughter-in-law who'd be like a daughter? You're a sweet, spontaneous person. I'd welcome you into my home. I'd thrive on you. I've wanted a daughter since before I married. But Marcus is a long-term liability and I'm not going to spend the remainder of my life funding his hospitalisations. My drawing room is already empty because of him. My bureau. My cabinets. Like him at the cost of your present happiness. Love him at the cost of your future happiness. Marry him at the cost of your eternal happiness. He is the single greatest problem in his own life. Until he realises that, he'll remain what he is: a medicated manic depressive with no real manhood.

FELICITY. There's nothing wrong with his manhood. When his dosage is reduced, he'll be fine.

MOTHER. I didn't mean that. I meant his manliness, not his . . . genital functions.

FELICITY. Why didn't you say manliness, then? Why did you say manhood?

MOTHER. Please don't do those sort of things in my home.

FELICITY. I don't think Marcus could make love in this house. It's an abattoir. (*The* MOTHER *sits heavily on the bed with a vacant expression on her face.*) I'm very sorry. I didn't mean that. It came out wrong. I was just hurt.

MOTHER. I'm not joyless. Not a joyless person. Far from it. But serious. Yes, I suppose. Serious. The night before my wedding, my mother told me that I'd been conceived during her honeymoon in Lourdes before the War. Not the first War, mind you. The second. So perhaps that's why I'm serious. Sometimes I think of my mum and my dad having their first dinner in Lourdes and looking out the window at the candlelight procession and the wheelchairs going by. (*Pause.*) Would you like some dust from the catacombs? (*Shows it.*)

FELICITY. Maybe another time.

MOTHER. Or a Padre Pio relic? Hmm?

FELICITY. I'm a bit of a black Protestant.

MOTHER. So am I. (*She drops them into the black bag.*)

ARTHUR (*enters by the door*). Black Protestant. That's obviously my cue.

FELICITY. How do.

MOTHER. Arthur, I never in my life knew why you were called Methodists. Now I do.

ARTHUR. Why's that, then?

MOTHER. Because you took charge of absolutely everything in the most methodical fashion. You should have been an undertaker.

ARTHUR. Well, it wasn't a pleasure, obviously, but it was a privilege.

MOTHER. And Rodney's ringing from Canada in the middle of the mass was most thoughtful.

ARTHUR. Poor timing, good intentions; same as his onlie begetter.

MOTHER. Yes.

ARTHUR. I'm off, so. And I meant what I said about the Dragon. *Jordan* would be a fine, strong name for a fine, strong boat. And a better one than the present, I should add. *Ripples* is not a racer's title.

MOTHER. Thank you. And I meant what I said about Jordan. He told me often how fond he was of your company. You were a father-figure to him.

ARTHUR (*moved*). Honoured. (*He bows.*)

MOTHER. Would you like to use the fire-escape? Whenever I look at it, I think of you.

ARTHUR. Clearing out that damn greenhouse has crippled my back. I'll take the stairs. To be continued! (*He leaves.*)

MOTHER (*pause*). Arthur.

FELICITY (*laughs*). I know.

MOTHER. What do you know?

FELICITY. Only that Arthur is . . . Arthur.

MOTHER. He's a fool but he's not a knave. (*Pause.*) I don't know what I'm doing, Felicity.

FELICITY. Would you rather leave it for now?

MOTHER (*more of* JORDAN's *clothes slip from her hands*). His smell is all over them.

FELICITY. Of course.

MOTHER. I think I'll go to my room for a moment.

FELICITY. Shall I . . . ? (*Indicates the clothes.*)

MOTHER. No. Leave everything.

She goes out and MARCUS *appears at the fire escape.*

MARCUS. Room service. (*In he comes and kisses her.*) You smell delicious. You're not to wash for a week. I love your smells.

FELICITY. Mad looney. Marcus the dark horse. (MARCUS *slides to his knees, presses his face against her sex and inhales it loudly.*) She loves you, Marcus. You're her child. But she won't take the initiative. She's too proud. (*She runs her hands through his hair.*) Will you be the first?

MARCUS. I've spent my whole life being the last. It's a hard habit to break.

FELICITY. I won't wash for a fortnight if you do.

MARCUS. She's going to have a complete nervous breakdown and I'll end up visiting her. If there is a God, he/she/it loves symmetry.

His arms move over her stomach and breasts. She ducks to kiss his wrists. They look at each other. Anthony enters.

FATHER ANTHONY. I'm sorry. The door was open.

FELICITY. No. Come in, Anthony.

MARCUS. You must be exhausted.

FATHER ANTHONY. A bit bushed. Like yourselves.

MARCUS. Actually, I haven't felt so awake for I don't know how long.

FATHER ANTHONY. That's because you're in the midst of an immense human experience.

FELICITY. Well, I could do without an immense human experience for the rest of my life.

FATHER ANTHONY. I could do without kitchen duty in the community house. But I'd better go.

MARCUS. What are you preparing for the psycho-geriatrics tonight?

FATHER ANTHONY. Jelly and sausages. Not necessarily in that order.

MARCUS. Whenever I'm committed, they teach me how to make apple tart all over again. I could show you.

FELICITY. I could show you how to make fresh fruit salad out of a tin. All you do is add alcohol.

MARCUS. The last time we ate together was in here. We got to tell the stories but not to share the food.

FATHER ANTHONY. We'll rise again.

MARCUS. Will we? Rise again, I mean?

FATHER ANTHONY. We will. Jordan will and you will and so will Felicity and your mother and even me.

FELICITY. What about Arthur?

FATHER ANTHONY. I'm not so sure about Methodists. It's a different trade union. (*He goes to the hostess trolley.*) I was looking for Jordan's shaver. Would you mind very much if I . . . ?

MARCUS. Of course not.

FATHER ANTHONY. You don't know what I'm –

MARCUS. Perhaps I do.

FATHER ANTHONY *taps soot from the shaver into a small envelope and puts it away into an inside pocket of his jacket.*

FATHER ANTHONY. He was very good to me, you know. (*Pause.*) He was a great Christian.

MARCUS. He was greatly interested in Christianity. Is that the same thing?

FATHER ANTHONY. I have double vision from all my studies. He had second sight from all his sufferings.

MARCUS. Anthony, organised religion drove Jordan out of his mind.

FATHER ANTHONY. Then he was even more like Jesus than I realised. (*He goes.*)

MARCUS. Anthony!

FELICITY (*to* MARCUS). Leave him alone.

MARCUS. I hate it when somebody gets the last word just by walking out. It's cheating. (*Calls.*) Anthony! Anthony!

He leaves and she follows him. Light is fading in the garden. After a few moments, the MOTHER *enters, barefoot as before. She's carrying a portable cassette recorder that she places on the floor beside the bed. She sits on the mattress and presses the play button with her toe.*

JORDAN'S VOICE. Mum, this is Marcus's doing. If you find it in lamentable taste, you know who to blame. He is, after all, the family scapegoat.

I'd like to think that you're listening to me in my own room with the windows wide open on a pretty afternoon and that you're wearing the dress – is it a dress or a frock? – which goes so well with those shoes. You know the ones.

Mum, I hope very much that, in the fullness of time, you and I will meet again. But I don't know. I don't know, Mum. I don't believe that you will find me in my death, like Thomas, Doubting Thomas, probing those holes with his rational, disgusted finger; but I do believe that you will find me in your pain, like Mary, was it, one of the Maries, who stood in a cemetery crying until her tears turned the graveyard into a garden.

I love you, Mum, and I thank you for being my mother, and I am afraid to go away from this world which is the only ground that I know. I've always felt that eternity is such a waste of time. But it may be that there will be a time and a place, beyond the two of us and beyond our lives, where you will recognise me as your son and I will recognise you as my mother. Please God, as they say.

In the meantime look after Marcus. You were made for each other. You were made from each other. If you bicker, I'll come back and go bump in the night.

As the MOTHER *sits thinking, an earlier recording of rock music starts to play on the tape. She reaches down slowly and turns it off. Then she lies down on the mattress with her head where* JORDAN*'s had been. She stares at the ceiling.* MARCUS *enters with letters in his hand and stands looking.*

MOTHER. I wanted it to be you.

MARCUS. I wish it had been.

MOTHER. You were always envious of him, but never as much as in the last two years.

MARCUS. Yes.

MOTHER. Are there worse things than dying and death?

MARCUS. Yes.

MOTHER. I know.

MARCUS. I wish you well. I wish you very well. I wish you exceeding well. I kiss the palms of your hands.

MOTHER (*laughs*). Books! What books are you reading now?

MARCUS. Letters. (*Shows them.*) The first sympathy letters.

MOTHER. What do they say?

MARCUS *seats himself in an armchair, more or less as he was at the start of the first scene.*

MARCUS. Dear Martha and Marcus.

MOTHER. Is that what it says?

MARCUS. That's how it starts.

MOTHER. It doesn't.

MARCUS. Yes, it does.

MOTHER. Imagine. (*She laughs.*) Read another.

MARCUS (*chooses another*). Dear Martha and Marcus.

MOTHER. No.

MARCUS. Yes.

MOTHER. Another.

MARCUS. Dear Marcus and Martha.

MOTHER. Show me. No. Don't show me. (*Pause.*) How does it end?

MARCUS (*turns the page*). Please don't feel that you have to answer this letter.

MOTHER. Imagine.

MARCUS. I can read them tomorrow.

MOTHER. Yes. (*Pause.*) Thank you.

MARCUS. Shall I leave you?

MOTHER. No.

MARCUS. Sure?

MOTHER. If you like.

MARCUS. All right. (*He continues sitting. She stares at the ceiling.*)

MOTHER. I found a stopwatch down the side of the bed.

MARCUS. Ahh.

MOTHER. When I was stripping it. A stopwatch. You wind it.

MARCUS. Not mine.

MOTHER. I thought philosophers went on about time. All the time.

MARCUS. It's Arthur's stopwatch. And Jordan's.

MOTHER. I love the sound of a clock. The tick tock of it. But a stopwatch. (*Pause.*) Arthur's stopwatch. And him with no sense of timing at all.

MARCUS. Would you not rest?

MOTHER. I am resting. I'm resting here.

MARCUS. Would you not rest better on your own bed?

MOTHER. You want to be alone in here?

MARCUS. I've never been alone in here. It's the only room in the house that isn't lonely.

MOTHER. I know. (*Silence.*) My eyes are at me. Dry, burning. As if there were sand in the pleats. Are the drops there?

MARCUS. Where?

MOTHER. Where do you think? On the trolley.

MARCUS. I suppose.

MOTHER. Get them for me.

MARCUS (*pause*). All right. (*He finds the bottle, brings it to her.*) There.

MOTHER. Do them for me. Would you?

MARCUS. You'd be better doing them yourself.

MOTHER. I can't. They run down my face. I look like I'm weeping.

MARCUS (*pause*). Lie still. Open. Open wide. (*He begins to put them in.*)

MOTHER. He was so patient. Wasn't he?

MARCUS. Don't look at me. Look at the ceiling.

MOTHER. Wasn't he?

MARCUS (*fierce*). Don't blink. (*Pause.*) Now the other. Wide. Open wide. Lie still. Stare at the ceiling. Not at me. (*Pause.*) Good. Good.

The window is almost dark. The MOTHER *lies on the mattress.* MARCUS *stands over her. The play ends.*

78

A Nick Hern Book

Communion first published in Great Britain and
the Republic of Ireland in 2002 as a paperback original
by Nick Hern Books, 14 Larden Road, London W3 7ST,
in association with the Abbey Theatre, Dublin

Communion copyright © 2002 by Aidan Mathews

Aidan Mathews has asserted his moral right to be identified
as the author of this work

Typeset by Country Setting, Kingsdown, Kent CT14 8ES
Printed by Bookmarque, Croydon, Surrey

A CIP catalogue record for this book is available from
the British Library

ISBN 1 85459 689 6

CAUTION All rights whatsoever in this play are strictly reserved.
Requests to reproduce the text in whole or in part should be
addressed to the publisher.

Amateur Performing Rights Applications for performance by
amateurs, including readings and excerpts, should be addressed to
the Performing Rights Manager, Nick Hern Books, 14 Larden Road,
London W3 7ST, *fax* +44 (020) 8735 0250, *e-mail*
info@nickhernbooks.demon.co.uk, except as follows:

Australia Dominie Drama, 8 Cross Street, Brookvale 2100,
fax (2) 9905 5209, *e-mail* dominie@dominie.com.au

New Zealand: Play Bureau, PO Box 420, New Plymouth,
fax (6) 753 2150, *e-mail* play.bureau.nz@xtra.co.nz

United States of America and Canada: A P Watt Ltd – as below.

Professional Performing Rights Application for performance by
professionals in any medium and in any language throughout the
world and for amateur rights in USA and Canada should be
addressed to A P Watt Ltd, 20 John Street, London, WC1N 2DR,
tel. (020) 7405 6774, *fax* (020) 7831 2154, *email* apw@apwatt.co.uk

No performance of any kind may be given unless a licence has
been obtained. Applications should be made before rehearsals
begin. Publication of this play does not necessarily indicate its
availability for amateur performance.